Second Edition

PRACTICAL
ACTION
RESEARCH
FOR CHANGE

RICHARD A. SCHMUCK

Foreword by Eleanor Perry

CORWIN PRESS
A SAGE Publications Company
Thousand Oaks, California

For information:

Corwin Press, Inc.
A Sage Publications Company
2455 Teller Road
Thousand Oaks, California 91320
www.corwinpress.com

Sage Publications Ltd.
1 Oliver's Yard
55 City Road
London EC1Y 1SP
United Kingdom

Sage Publications India Pvt. Ltd.
B-42, Panchsheel Enclave
Post Box 4109
New Delhi 110 017 India

Printed in the United States of America.

Library of Congress Cataloging-in-Publication Data
Schmuck, Richard A.
Practical action research for change / Richard A. Schmuck.— 2nd ed.
      p. cm.
Includes bibliographical references and index.
ISBN 1-4129-3858-9 (cloth) — ISBN 1-4129-3859-7 (pbk.)
   1. Action research in education—Handbooks, manuals, etc. I. Title.
LB1028.24.S45 2006

370.7'2—dc22   2005037813

06 07 08 09 10   10 9 8 7 6 5 4 3 2 1

Acquisitions Editor:	Cathy Hernandez
Editorial Assistant:	Charline Wu
Project Editor:	Kate Peterson
Copy Editor:	Barbara Coster
Typesetter:	C&M Digitals (P) Ltd.
Indexer:	Richard A. Schmuck
Cover Designer:	Audrey Snodgrass

Contents

Foreword

Journal entry—November 5, 2005

A long time ago, Richard Schmuck told me, "Ellie, you must learn to turn frustrations into problems, because problems can be solved, frustrations can't." Oh, how his words changed my life—and no doubt the lives of thousands of educators nationally and internationally!

I remember when I first met him. I was a doctoral student at the University of Oregon in 1990 laden with a great deal of baggage. After many years as an educator, I left teaching to explore a career in business. The longer I stayed away from education, the more my heart ached to work with students again. When I came back to the classroom after a ten-year absence, something was different. I couldn't decide what. Had the kids changed? the parents? my colleagues? or had *I* changed as I entered midlife? Why were the students so undisciplined? Where were the parents? Why were my fellow teachers on the phone selling real estate during their planning periods? Where was my youthful enthusiasm I had years before?

- I struggled because I simply did not have the skills to be a reflective practitioner. Indeed, I never even considered journaling. Was that like keeping a professional diary?
- I did not have focused strategies to analyze problems. STP? I thought that was something my husband used in the car!
- I certainly had no idea where to start to improve my situation through self-study. Wasn't research something somebody else did from the outside in rather than the inside out?

Then I met Dick.

At the University of Oregon he taught me how to search for self-knowledge. As he does in this second edition of his book *Practical Action Research for Change,* he gave me the skills and knowledge related to the three components of continuous improvement. First, I learned to practice reflective thinking to get a better understanding of situations I faced and to prepare myself for new ways to take action. Second, I became a problem solver deeply entrenched in organizational development—a systematic way to create planned change. Then he introduced me to an incredibly powerful tool—action research.

Action research is a way for people within an organization to study their own situations individually and collectively, try new practices, evaluate those innovations, adjust, and try again. It is one big cycle of continuous improvement.

Action research is something we've done for years in our classrooms, schools, districts, and beyond. What we lacked was the formal structure to work methodically through issues. Dick gives us that structure in *Practical Action Research for Change*. I suppose it's like when the Good Witch told Dorothy that she didn't really need the ruby red slippers. She always had the power—she just needed to realize it. *Practical Action Research for Change* helps us realize the power within us to make education better for our children, teachers, staff, parents, and communities.

Action research certainly empowered me ten years ago when I was a school principal. I introduced my teachers and staff to the concept. The process became contagious. The more they learned, the more they wanted to know. Together we identified our current *Situation*, set specific *Targets* we wanted to reach, and designed the *Paths* we wanted to take to attain our goals. Action research became a way of life in our school. Our culture changed from a hornet's nest of complainers to a collaborative community of problem solvers.

Today action research is even timelier for educators. We are in a critical age of assessment and accountability. The federally mandated No Child Left Behind Act challenges educators to make continuous improvement based on data-driven decisions. Who best to collect that data than the people who live within the schoolhouse walls? *Practical Action Research for Change* details how to carry out proactive and responsive studies that inspire innovations and tackle sticky problems that need fixing. Educators must take control of their situations by formally studying them if they wish to control the outcomes.

In *Practical Action Research for Change* we learn how to control outcomes through example. Dick uses many easy-to-read cases showing how conducting action research provides insight into achieving educational goals. For example, in this second edition he draws on the work of students in the Arizona State University Leadership for Educational Entrepreneurs (LEE) program I founded and direct. LEE is an innovative, nationally recognized master's degree that bridges the MEd and MBA degrees. I specifically designed LEE for charter school leaders who need both education and business skills to promote student achievement successfully. *Practical Action Research for Change* showcases proactive and responsive studies conducted by the first cohort of LEE Fellows under the tutelage of Dr. Schmuck. Using the systematic data collection detailed in his book, those practitioner-scholars now boast of making a positive difference for more than 300,000 children nationwide.

We are enormously indebted to Richard Schmuck. His dedication to teaching action research is unparalleled. He captures the spirit of his classroom in the second edition of *Practical Action Research for Change*. For the educators Dick has taught, they will recognize his special way of entwining direct instruction with practical examples and journaling. For the educators yet to come, *Practical Action Research for Change* is a book they must read if they are serious about making a difference for kids.

Eleanor Martino Perry, PhD
Associate Professor
Director, Leadership for Educational Entrepreneurs
College of Teacher Education and Leadership
Arizona State University

Preface

With this book I teach you how to create your own meaningful action research in your classroom, school, and district. Hence the word practical in the title. To do action research, you use scientific methods to learn how well you are carrying out a practice new to you or to get in touch with your students' wishes for you to use new practices. When you do action research with your students continually and cyclically, you have attained a high level of professional maturity, the state of continuous improvement.

The hardest challenge of action research is getting started. In the first two chapters, I teach you how to get ready to do your own action research. I present information about two conditions of your readiness: (1) serious reflection on your own professional practice during which you focus on nagging frustrations and think about alternative practices and useful data to collect and (2) thoughtful use of a problem-solving method to convert your frustrations into solvable problems. For both introspective activities I offer specific concepts, procedures, and techniques to organize and systematize your preparation for action research.

Once you determine a focus for your action research, prepare a formal project plan. To help you implement action research, I give information and examples of its models, phases, and steps. To obtain sufficient knowledge to do action research well, you must read Chapters 3–6. From those four chapters, you will obtain practical knowledge about how to do action research. Among other things you will learn how to (1) distinguish action research from traditional research and know how the two overlap, (2) search for knowledge about new practices and useful research methods, (3) create research procedures tailored to your situation, (4) determine whether the proactive or responsive model is more appropriate for your project, (5) carry out every step of both models, and (6) cope with possible obstacles and pitfalls.

After you have mastered the ability to collaborate with your own students in doing action research, I believe you will be ready to explore projects larger in scope. Cooperative action research can occur among groups of administrators, teachers, specialists, classified personnel, students, parents, board members, and other community stakeholders. It is implemented at different system levels, ranging from one-on-one partnerships to statewide networks of educators and stakeholders. A significant difference between your own project and a larger cooperative effort is that the latter requires complex group-dynamics skills to be effective. So that you can take leadership in carrying out effective cooperative action research, I teach you how to apply specific group skills and offer illustrative case studies of many types.

I end where some critics think I should have started, with a historical discussion of prominent scholars who have written about the origins and growth of action research. I have not heeded their advice, because I believe that after you have a clear understanding of how to do your own action research and how to communicate well with others in cooperative action research, you will become receptive to the ideas of those scholars and be motivated to read their works.

A chapter-by-chapter summary follows.

Chapter 1 teaches you how to reflect on your future, past, and present professional practices, offering questions and techniques to use in obtaining professional self-knowledge. Reflection offers a means to pinpoint a focus for your action research. To enhance the quality of your reflectiveness, the chapter explains ways to use solitary dialogue and personal journals. It describes how reflection can facilitate continuous professional improvement and presents several tools to use in thinking your way into your own action research.

Chapter 2 explains how reflection, problem solving, and action research serve as the three faces of your continuous improvement as an educator. It presents a seven-step problem-solving procedure along with an example of how a high school teacher successfully used it. It delineates differences between action and traditional research, points out the overlap between them, and describes a case study about how another high school teacher carried out action research in one of his classes.

Chapter 3 discusses action research: the contemporary need for it, a working definition of it, the relevance of group dynamics to its effectiveness, and the phases and steps of the proactive and responsive models. Now you should start your own initial plan for action research.

Chapter 4 explains how you can use research methods in action research. After a discussion of data collection procedures, it offers specific examples of questionnaires, interviews, observations, and documents. It addresses the special issues of validity, reliability, and precision; helps you avoid pitfalls that will occur; and presents do's and don'ts about the ethics of action research.

Chapter 5 explains how to conduct proactive action research, and Chapter 6 does the same for responsive action research. Those two chapters are the heart of the book. Now you should be ready to choose one of the two models to carry out an action research plan of your own.

Chapter 7 introduces the complex group dynamics of cooperative action research, and Chapter 8 describes the different types of cooperative action research in schools, districts, and communities. Now you should see how you can assume leadership with colleagues in carrying out action research on a larger scale.

Chapter 9 discusses the democratic philosophy undergirding educational action research. Although the ends of action research are higher student learning and strengthened professional practice, the means are democratic group procedures. The chapter goes on to describe the contributions of 15 prominent authors in the history of action research, recommends your reading Figure 9.6, The Educator's Essential Action Research Library (a list of ten seminal publications), and explains how the history of educational action research has developed into the teacher-research movement.

To help you apply the book's contents to your own situation, I end every chapter with personal journal-writing assignments.

I stand behind this book's organization and chapter sequence by returning to one of my caveats: "The hardest challenge of action research is getting started." The best place to start meaningful action research is inside your mind by reflecting on your own professional practice. Get in touch with and listen to your own internal voice; act out the dialogues within you. Pinpoint your frustrations; convert them into solvable problems. Move on to do well-planned action research, tailored to your own situation. Take leadership in cooperating with colleagues to do action research in your own school, community, and state. Also, read the intelligent writing of published scholars to broaden and deepen your understanding and commitment to action research. Let us hope that by reading this book and related publications, you will become a more mature professional educator.

Richard A. Schmuck

Acknowledgments

I thank the thousands of dedicated educators with whom I have collaborated and cooperated during the last 45 years. In particular, I thank educators who studied action research with me in

- The University of Oregon's Master's and Doctoral Program (1992–2005)
- Lewis and Clark's Doctoral Program in Educational Leadership (2004)
- Jackson State University's Education Faculty (2000–2005)
- Arizona State University–West's LEE (Leadership for Educational Entrepreneurs) Program in the College of Education (2002–2006)

I thank many of those thousands of educators who read the first edition, gave me advice for improvements in its organization and content, and offered creative ideas about journal-writing assignments to make the book's concepts, research methods, and action plans more practical to adult learners.

I also thank seven educators, recruited by Corwin Press to act as constructive critics, for their helpful reviews. I used many of their ideas in preparing this second edition.

I am especially thankful for the continued intellectual stimulation and affective support of Patricia Schmuck, my colleague, friend, lover, and partner of nearly 50 years.

PUBLISHER'S ACKNOWLEDGMENTS

Corwin Press gratefully acknowledges the contributions of the following reviewers:

Elizabeth F. Day, Sixth-Grade Teacher
Mechanicville Middle School, Mechanicville, NY

Clara Fitzpatrick, Professor, Educational Studies
Columbia College Chicago, Chicago, IL

Nina L. Greenwald, Professor and Director, Critical and Creative Thinking
    Graduate Program
University of Massachusetts, Boston, MA

Gail R. Luera, Assistant Professor, Science Education
University of Michigan–Dearborn, Dearborn, MI

About the Author

Richard A. Schmuck is Professor Emeritus at the University of Oregon, where he chaired dissertations of 132 doctoral students from all parts of the world. He taught thousands of other educators worldwide about action research, group dynamics, and organization development.

He has served on the faculties of the University of Michigan, Temple University, and Leuven University (Belgium), was the first President of the International Association for the Study of Cooperation in Education, and is a Visiting Professor at Arizona State University–West.

He is the author of 20 books and 190 articles. His best known book is *Group Processes in the Classroom* (with Patricia Schmuck), in its eighth edition. One article about school development won the Douglas McGregor Award for outstanding applications of behavioral science to practical affairs. One book, published by Corwin Press (*Small Districts, Big Problems*), won the outstanding research award of the National Rural Education Association.

He received the Stevens Award from the Northwest Women in Educational Administration to honor his support of "women in administration" and his "commitment to equity, justice, and democracy," and he received the Campbell Lifetime Achievement Award from the University Council on Educational Administration for "superior scholarship, distinguished service, and recognized international leadership" and "to celebrate an extraordinary and generous career."

At 70 years, he teaches, consults, and writes. Along with his spouse of 47 years, he lives at the foot of Mount Hood, in Hood River, Oregon, where he has served for 7 years on the United Way board.

1

Reflective Professional Practice

Thought takes place as internal conversation, having developed through social processes.

—George Herbert Mead (1934)

Who expects small things to survive when even the largest get lost. People forget years and remember moments. Seconds and symbols are left to sum things up.

—Ann Beattie (1986)

Fixing your mind on how your professional practice has affected your students can enhance your wish for self-improvement and get you on the road to action research. To get ready to do action research, reflect on your own professional practice. Professional reflection is self-focused meditation that includes visualizing where you are, where you have been, and where you might go. Like reading a map upon entering a college campus, professional reflection helps you see where you are now (X marks the spot) and alternative paths to reach other campus high spots you might wish to visit later or have visited before. In striving to become a better practitioner, you must move from intelligent assessments of where you are at present to reflect on how to use past and future strategies to realize planned change.

Although professional reflection calls for silence, the social psychologist G. H. Mead (1934) believed that an integral association exists between thinking and social interaction and therefore that reflection is a sort of solitary conversation or internal dialogue. Ann Beattie (1986), the novelist and my favorite short story writer, pointed to an incongruity between what we expect of memory and what actually occurs. To paraphrase her, we focus our memories on poignant momentary events rather than on accumulations of large blocks of events over time. By getting in touch with your internal dialogues and by remembering a few poignant moments with your students, you can begin to fix on a focus for action research.

REFLECTIONS OF THE FUTURE, PAST, AND PRESENT

The philosopher Martin Heidegger (1962) posited that at all moments of thought and reflection, we dwell either in the future, the past, or the present. Unfortunately, most of us are not thoughtful about differentiating among the three states of time. Thus you who do not think deeply about the future do not measure the results and outcomes of your actions, you who do not reflect critically on the past are not readying yourselves for improvement, and you who do not think of what you are doing in the present cannot often see what to do next.

You think about your future practice when you plan a lesson, put up a bulletin board, design an instructional strategy, or rehearse a behavioral skill. When learning to play the trumpet in the sixth grade, my music teacher prodded me to go over the notes and fingering in my mind before I played. In high school, our football coach told us to rehearse offensive plays in our minds before the games. In freshman English in college, I was assigned to read *Think Before You Write* (Leary and Smith 1951), and my sophomore speech instructor urged me to visualize my audience in my mind's eye before starting my presentation.

Now, as a professor emeritus, I still do not enter the classroom without a teaching plan, nor do I carry out research or consultation without guiding questions and an explicit design for action. For teachers and students alike, reflecting about future behaviors and foreseeing outcomes are essential and necessary stepping-stones to effective action. See Figure 1.1 for an example of a teacher reflecting on the future.

You can also benefit from fixing your mind on your past plans and behaviors, how those plans unfolded, how your behaviors came across to the students, and what happened as consequences. Serious reflection on past practices helps you gain competence, mastery, and understanding, which serve as your foundations of psychological strength when facing the next challenge or a similar event.

Many years after freshman composition, I learned from experience about the power and usefulness of spontaneous, free writing. I learned to start an article, a chapter, or a proposal for funding by rapidly jotting down words, phrases, and clauses without allowing my pen to leave the paper or my fingers to stray far from the keyboard. Then, after reflecting on what James Joyce called the "streams of consciousness" in my initial jottings, I wrote sentences, paragraphs, and outlines. Later, after more analytical reflections, I prepared drafts—writing-reflecting-rewriting-reflecting-rewriting—until I had developed my voice and was satisfied with the lucidity of my statements.

In learning to think clearly about the past, it took me quite a few years to appreciate the power of debriefing—a procedure used by diplomats or soldiers when they reflect upon and mentally assess the conduct and results of a mission. Debriefing can

Figure 1.1   Reflecting on the Future

A teacher is about to meet with the parents of a child who has been difficult to work with during class discussion. She works through the following questions to prepare herself.

What are the disruptive behaviors?

- The student does not listen well, often interrupts other students, and is sometimes discourteous to the teacher.

When does the child disrupt the class?

- The student is most disruptive after lunch.

What are some possible reactions of the parents?

- I wonder if my child is getting too much sugar at lunch.
- Perhaps my child is too advanced for your class and is bored.
- My child thinks you single her out and pick on her.

How will I respond to each of these reactions?

- Maybe we could alter the student's diet over the next two weeks and see if her social behavior improves.
- Your child's assessment scores in reading and math show that . . . [Have assessment scores handy.]
- Your child does not seem to have a close friend in class. Can you help me understand that?
- I reprimand your child only when she is disruptive. [Show parents your written record of disturbances.]
- I reward your child at least two or three times a week. [Show parents your written record of rewards.]
- Let's brainstorm together about some new ways we might try to relate to your child.

apply as well to playing musical instruments or to participating in athletic games as it does to making speeches, teaching classes, carrying out research and consultations, or implementing missions. For all of those pursuits, serious reflection in the aftermath can help you gain competence, mastery, and understanding. Take action first, then think critically and systematically about the effects of those actions before acting again. Doing so will help you zero in on a focus for action research. See Figure 1.2 for an example of a teacher reflecting on the past.

Heidegger pointed out that because our minds typically wander between past and future reveries, thinking in the present is the least used form of reflection. In fact, the most challenging type of reflection is thinking about your present behavior, which calls for you to focus on the here and now instead of the there and then. Reflecting effectively on the future or the past entails segmenting your thoughts into distinguishable episodes to consider the interrelated parts. Reflecting effectively in the present, in contrast, calls for moment-to-moment shifts between doing and thinking and thinking and doing.

In his theory about the development of a self-concept, Mead (1934) conceived of your "I" as your behaving self in spontaneous emission prior to your reflecting on it and your "me" as that part of yourself that you reflect upon. In other words, your "me" is your self-perception from moment to moment. Reflecting effectively on your present behavior requires tight coupling between your "I" and your "me." While behaving, you simultaneously introspect about your behavior. You catch yourself in the act of behaving. Your behavior and your reflection on it happen virtually at the

Figure 1.2 Reflecting on the Past

A teacher thinks about her meetings with parents in the past.

- The last few times I confronted parents about the disruptive behavior of their child, I did not have in mind enough concrete examples of the disruptive behavior.
- The parents saw me as picking on their child. They did not understand how their child's classmates were reacting toward the disruptive behavior.
- I did not connect their child's behavior to the negative effects it was having on other students' learning, nor did I connect it to their child's performance in reading and math.
- I became defensive, and I did not invite the parents to join me in brainstorming alternative actions for each of us to take in trying to change the child's disruptive behavior.
- I do not want to make those same mistakes again.

---

same time. Reflecting well in the present, a hard task at best, requires you to be sensitive and insightful about the nonverbal reactions of your students. You can find no better launching pad for action research than to become conscious of your students' nonverbal reactions to your instruction.

I think that I am best at reflecting in the present when I engage in one-on-one advising, counseling, or conferring. I can monitor the other person's reactions to my actions and quickly regulate what I say or do next, according to the instant insight I get about the other's changing mental state. As the number of people I simultaneously relate to increases, the challenges I experience in effectively reflecting in the here and now also increases. I am forced to reflect more on the past or future, even as I try to stay in the present. Nevertheless, as I teach, consult, or convene committee meetings, I do strive to remain alert and vigilant to others' current reactions to my verbal and nonverbal behaviors. I know too that a sound way for me to learn about the others' reactions is through action research. See Figure 1.3 for an example of a teacher reflecting on the present.

Although reflections on the future, past, and present are very important skills for you to master to increase your effectiveness, they cannot in themselves solve your problems. Each of us has a limited capacity to improve our practice through reflection alone. We can use reflection to fine-tune our practice but not to create new and innovative practice. The effectiveness of your reflections can be significantly enhanced by scientific inquiry—the systematic collection and analysis of data from your students about your practice. By using research methods, you can move beyond your solitary dialogue to engage your students in "public dialogue" about their experiences in your classroom.

REFLECTIVE EDUCATORS SEEK SELF-KNOWLEDGE

Socrates, the Greek philosopher of 400 B.C., employed a question-and-answer teaching procedure to help his students achieve self-knowledge (read Taylor 1956). I offer my own rendition of the Socratic method to help you know your educator self better. I start with the metaphor of the runner.

Think of yourself as a runner in the past, present, and future: one leg is ahead into the future, the other leg behind in the past, your torso poised in between in the

Figure 1.3   Reflecting on the Present

The teacher meets with the parents of a disruptive student.

She stands as the parents enter the room, aware that she must reach out to them with her right hand while maintaining a broad smile on her face. She invites them to sit down and brings her own chair up close to theirs without a table or desk between them. She searches their faces and physical postures for cues to their comfort and readiness to cooperate. She concentrates on being direct, using only a few sentences, and on maintaining eye contact. Are they looking at her eyes? Do they nod their heads? She looks for pursed lips and listens for sighs of frustration. As she moves the discussion toward cooperative brainstorming of solutions, she is aware of extending her arms out toward them to signal a cooperative discussion. She is aware of using the word *we* several times. As the parents leave, she walks with them to the door, again extending her right hand to shake theirs and aware that she has a smile on her face.

---

here and now. Yet, as one whole runner, you move gracefully from moment to moment toward your goal.

As a reflective educator in search of self-knowledge, think like a runner as you strive to achieve your professional goals and ponder Socratic questions about your present, past, and future throughout your career. In the present, ask yourself, "What am I doing now? How am I acting? How am I living my values? Are my current actions congruent with my cherished beliefs? Am I practicing what I preach? Does my current behavior offer a standard for my students to imitate?"

You can help yourself answer those questions by becoming more conscious of your own self-concept and of your beliefs and values about human nature.

You can grow toward a keener awareness of yourself by writing in a personal journal about

- The central aspects of your self-concept
- The core concepts that guide your explanations of why students behave as they do
- The most important values or desirable ends that guide your professional behavior

Looking to the past, ask yourself, "How did I develop to be who I am now? Which of my past experiences had the most influence on my current beliefs, values, and behaviors? Who were the most powerful role models of my youth and early adulthood?"

In your personal journal, write about

- Your reasons for wanting to be a teacher (or be in another role in education)
- The characteristics of your favorite teacher or administrator
- Influential people, groups, and events in your life

Fixing your mind on the present, seek to understand how your current practices affect students, parents, and colleagues. Ask yourself, "How am I coming across to those I serve? What are my students' perceptions of my practices? What are my students learning and feeling? How do my students' parents assess me as a teacher or as an administrator? How do my professional peers see me as a colleague?"

If you truly wish to obtain self-knowledge, go beyond writing answers to the above queries in your journal and collect scientific data to help answer them. Armed with data from your students, you will become even more concerned about how you can do things better in the future. You will ask yourself, "What changes might help me better achieve my professional goals? How can I increase consistency between my values and my behaviors? What changes should I make in my concepts about what motivates student behavior to get ready for future challenges?"

In your personal journal, complete the following sentences:

- As a teacher or administrator, I prefer to influence students with the following behaviors: _____
  _____.

- Significant aspects of my current vision for education are _____
  _____.

- When I apply for my next position in education, I will state the following things about myself to highlight my capacity and values as an effective educator: _____
  _____.

Figure 1.4 is an excerpt from one reflective educator's journal.

Figure 1.4   Journal Entry

Reflecting on the Future

- The central aspects of my self-concept: active, athletic, extrovert
- The core concepts that guide my explanations of human behavior: choosing among alternatives fosters involvements and commitment
- The most important values or desirable ends that guide my professional behavior: strive to increase students' prosocial skills

Reflecting on the Past

- My reasons for wanting to be a teacher: to give students of today the wonderful gifts I received from the great teachers who taught me
- The characteristics of my favorite teachers: caring, clear, supportive, flexible, understanding
- Influential people in my life: my 12th-grade English teacher

Reflecting on the Present

- As an educator, I prefer to influence people with the following behaviors: active listening, succinct statements, supportive feedback.
- Significant aspects of my vision for education are that cooperative learning and peer tutoring can help develop students' prosocial skills.
- When I apply for a new position in education, I will state the following thing about myself to highlight my capacity and values as an effective educator: I adapt my teaching strategies to student learning styles.

THE SEARCH FOR SELF-KNOWLEDGE LEADS TO SOLITARY DIALOGUE

About 2,000 years after Socrates, William Shakespeare created theatrical soliloquies to express the conflicted and unsettling reflections of such memorable characters as Hamlet, Lady Macbeth, and King Richard III. The reflective-thinking technique of solitary dialogue, similar to what Shakespeare called "soliloquy," is a conversation between two sides of the inner self. As I said earlier, G. H. Mead likened human thought or reflection to internal conversation or to solitary dialogue. Use solitary dialogue to get a better understanding of yourself and to ready yourself for new actions.

One type of solitary dialogue that could be useful to you is a conversation between your frustrated past self and your hopeful future self. Your frustrated past self uses verbs such as *couldn't, defended, didn't, feared, worried, rejected, resisted, struggled,* and *wanted.* Your hopeful future self uses verbs such as *can, search, seek, strive, want, will,* and *yearn for.* Figure 1.5 offers an example of a reflective educator working through an inner conflict with solitary dialogue.

Another type of solitary dialogue is a conversation between your past courageous self and your future doubting self. Your courageous self uses phrases such as "I bit the bullet and acted, challenged, even though I was in the minority, confronted and spoke up, mastered my fear, and succeeded in overcoming reluctance and reticence." Your doubting self uses phrases such as "I might fall on my face, will forget and leave out important points, will get stage fright and look foolish, and won't be accepted or respected by others."

Other types of solitary dialogues that you might try are conversations between your tough and tender selves, task-centered and person-centered selves, pushing and pulling selves, caring and challenging selves, worried and laid-back selves, convergent and divergent selves, and creative and conservative selves. Develop a solitary dialogue that is tailored to who you are and what most you want to accomplish with your students.

Figure 1.5   Solitary Dialogue

The following is an example of a solitary dialogue with the future and past selves:

PAST SELF: When I felt fear and frustration like this before, I didn't listen carefully to others. I defended myself, jumped to the wrong conclusions, and resisted a reasonable compromise.

FUTURE SELF: I will remain cool when under fire. I will strive to listen. I will use paraphrasing and impression checking before seeking to get my own points across. I will try not to project my feelings onto others.

PAST SELF: That's easier said than done. In the heat of anger, I couldn't paraphrase, and when I struggled to check my impressions of others' feelings, I came across as judgmental.

FUTURE SELF: The next time will be different. I am maturing more and more every day. I will strive to let others know that I do understand and empathize with their feelings, even when I disagree with their points of view.

SELF-KNOWLEDGE AND SOLITARY DIALOGUE LEAD TO PROFESSIONAL MATURITY

As you reflect on your past, present, and future to develop self-knowledge, and as you engage in solitary dialogue, your professional perspectives become more mature. Immature educators focus often on their survival as teachers or administrators. As the immature have experiences and think about what they hope to achieve, their preoccupation with themselves decreases, and they search outside themselves for clues about their students' or colleagues' reactions. Later, with more experience in checking others' reactions, those who feel secure become primarily concerned with outcomes and results.

In their pathbreaking book *Change in Schools* (1987), Hall and Hord wrote about the concerns of teachers who face the challenge of trying new practices in their classrooms. They found that when prodded to change, teachers are concerned first about themselves ("Will I be able to carry out the new practice well?"), later they become concerned about others ("Will my students react well or poorly to the new practice?"), and still later they become concerned about results ("Will the new practice result in better student outcomes?"). Hall and Hord found four levels of concerns about self, three levels of concerns about others, and three levels of concerns about results, as shown in Figure 1.6.

MATURE EDUCATORS TRY TO IMPROVE CONTINUALLY

As a mature educator, you are concerned with continuous improvement in achieving results or in reaching valued outcomes. To reach your desired results, try to segment

Figure 1.6   The Maturing Educator's Three Levels of Concern

Focus on Self	Focus on Others	Focus on Results
Concern 1: Personal security, status, and comfort: Can I survive in this job?	Concern 5: Others' perceptions of behavior, values, and plans: What are others' perceptions of my professional behavior?	Concern 8: Immediate applicability of teachings: What can others do as a consequence of my having taught them?
Concern 2: Professional self-esteem: Do I feel good about myself in this job?	Concern 6: Others' attitudes about behavior: What are others' attitudes about my professional behavior?	Concern 9: Future applicability of teachings: What lasting effects have I had on my students?
Concern 3: Personal values, hopes, aspirations, and plans: Can I make a career in education? Can I achieve my life's goals as an educator?	Concern 7: Effect of behavior on others: What are others' nonverbal and verbal reactions to my professional behavior?	Concern 10: Contribution to society: What long-lasting contributions do my students make to improving our community, nation, and world?
Concern 4: Professional behavior: Are my professional actions congruent with my values and plans?		

your planning, acting, and evaluating into the following ten stages. This sequence of introspective stages will help you move from reflection to action research.

Stage 1: Assess the Situation

Your situation is made up of the people you interact with in the present. In particular, focus on your current thoughts about your students' attitudes and capabilities. Also look at surrounding social events that are helping or hindering student learning.

Stage 2: Set Clear Goals

With thoughtful reflection on your own values and beliefs, you can set goals or targets or objectives. For example, your goal might be for your students to internalize some new knowledge or skill, to act in certain new ways, to develop particular attitudes or values, or to view themselves in new ways.

Stage 3: Brainstorm Action Strategies

To move from your present situation toward goal achievement, use your knowledge and experience to create such action strategies as revised lesson plans, curriculum designs, and instructional procedures. Reflect on your past learning experiences in college courses and inservice workshops; conduct problem-solving discussions with colleagues, consultants, and college professors in the present.

Stage 4: Implement Action Plans

Carry out an action strategy that you created in Stage 3 on a trial basis.

Stage 5: Monitor Your Own Actions

Monitoring your new actions calls for you to reflect in the here and now. Strive to make moment-to-moment shifts between doing and thinking by becoming sensitive to nonverbal reactions of your students.

Stage 6: Assess Others' Reactions

Now think about how you might collect data to assess your students' perceptions and attitudes about your new actions. What research methods might you use?

Stage 7: Evaluate What Others Have Learned

Think about how you might collect data to answer questions such as "Have my students developed the qualities that I was looking for when I set the goals in Stage 2? Are the outcomes or results that I am getting desirable? Have there been any unexpected, undesirable outcomes?"

Stage 8: Confront Yourself With the Results

Compare your desired goals of Stage 2 with the kind of data you might have collected in Stage 7. Look for agreement or disagreement between the two. Confront yourself with ways that you have been effective or ineffective.

Stage 9: Reflect on Actions to Take Next

Here you virtually repeat Stage 3. This time, either fine-tune the action plan you trial-tested in Stage 4 or make a more significant modification if that plan did not work well. If the latter seems appropriate, engage colleagues, consultants, or college professors in problem-solving discussions.

Stage 10: Assess the New Situation and Set New Goals

You have come full circle to take a fresh look at your situation and to set new, more achievable goals. Once you set new goals, recycle through the stages again and again. This is the mental frame of continuous professional improvement.

USING THE TOOLS OF REFLECTION TO MOVE TOWARD ACTION RESEARCH

Reflection and action research are two sides of the coin of planned change. By using both, you demonstrate your professional maturity and your value for continuous improvement.

Use four tools of reflection—force field analysis, situation-target-path (STP) concepts, brainstorming versus critical thinking, and self-confrontation—to move toward your own action research.

According to Kurt Lewin (1951), the grandfather of action research, every social situation is in quasiequilibrium, a state of unsteady balance between the actions of opposing forces. Use force field analysis, as shown in Figure 1.7, to obtain a fuller understanding of what might be done to improve your situation.

Visualize your current situation as being made up of a field of facilitating and restraining forces. The facilitating forces are helping you move toward your goals, the desired state on the right of the field, while the restraining forces are hindering

Figure 1.7   Force Field Analysis

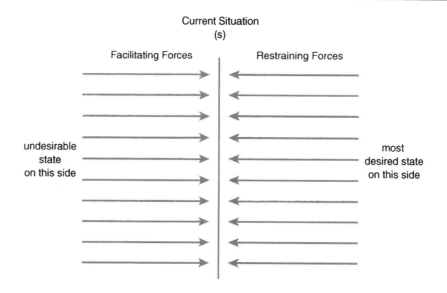

your getting to the right and pushing you toward the left of the field, toward the undesirable state.

Once you have listed five to ten forces that characterize your situation on each side of the field, you are ready to focus on topics for your action research. You want either to increase the facilitating forces or decrease the restraining forces. So think creatively about how you might act to do that.

Lewin (1948) taught that it often is better to focus on reducing the restraining forces than on increasing the facilitating forces. My advice is for you to do just that. Think of a focus for your action research that would work toward a reduction in the power of some of the restraining forces in your situation.

A second tool of reflection to help you move toward action research is my own STP paradigm (see Schmuck and Runkel 1994).

In Figure 1.8, note that S stands for your current situation, T stands for your target, and P stands for your path, plan, procedure, project, or proposal. Simply put, your action research will focus either on your S (collect data to understand better your situation) or on your P (collect data to understand your plan's effectiveness).

Force field analysis and the STP paradigm can be integrated. You can conceive of your current S as a field of facilitating and restraining forces held in quasiequilibrium. You create Ps to reduce the restraining forces or to add to the facilitating forces. By combining the two tools, you might develop a deeper understanding of your S, thereby giving you a broader perspective for creating an appropriate P.

A third tool to help you move toward successful action research is to distinguish between brainstorming and critical thinking. Brainstorming helps foster creativity and opens your irrational and intuitive selves. Critical thinking helps foster decision making and opens your rational and objective selves. Both take on a critical function in action research. You should know how to tell them apart and how to do both. In fact, students too should know how to apply the two in classroom discussions and problem solving.

A fourth tool to help you move toward action research is the skill of self-confrontation. Self-confrontation takes place when you are clear about what you value, and you gather data to assess how true you are being to those values. As gaps between your values and assessments arise, you will often feel cognitive dissonance and wish for change to take place. A fundamental ingredient of action research is clarity of values. To zero in on a focus for your action research, try to become super clear about your core values. Then you will want to move from concerns about yourself to concerns about results. Figure 1.9 summarizes the developmental relationships between self-focus, concerns with others' reactions, and the search for results.

Figure 1.8   STP Concepts

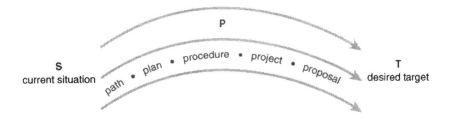

Figure 1.9   From Reflection to Action Research

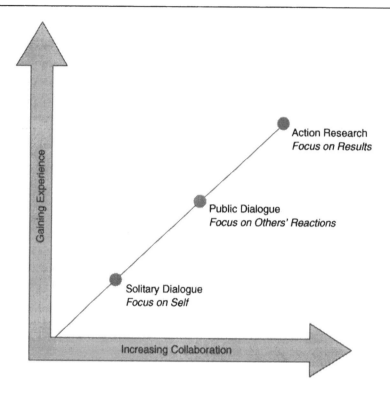

Know Thyself

Use the following sentence stems to reflect on who you are:

- The central parts of my self-concept are ______________________________

  ______________________________.

- The core concepts that guide my explanations of human behavior are ______________________________

  ______________________________.

- The most important values or ends that guide my professional behavior are ______________________________

  ______________________________.

- My reasons for wanting to be a teacher are ______________________________

  ______________________________.

- The characteristics of my favorite teacher are ______________________________

  ______________________________.

- The characteristics of influential people in my life are ______________________________

  ______________________________.

- As an educator, I prefer to influence students with the following behaviors: ______________________________

  ______________________________.

- Significant aspects of my vision for education are ______________________________

  ______________________________.

- When I apply for a new position in education, I will state the following things about myself to highlight my capacity and values as an effective educator: ______________________________

  ______________________________.

✖ Solitary Dialogue

Think of a challenge you face, will face, or have faced. Write a solitary dialogue to get your values and thoughts in order. Alternate between your past self and future self or between your tough self and your tender self, and so forth.

_____ Self:

_____ Self:

_____ Self:

_____ Self:

_____ Self:

_____ Self:

_____ Self:

_____ Self:

✳ Reflections

Reflect on Chapter 1 by answering the following questions:

1. Do I use a form of reflection now?

2. How might I use reflection more effectively?

3. How can I make solitary dialogue work for me?

4. How might I use the force field analysis?

5. How might I use the STP?

6. What are some of my concerns as a maturing professional?

7. How might I use the ten stages of maturing educators trying to improve continually?

8. What topics for my own action research come to mind?

Educators and Continuous Improvement

*Every teacher should have some regular and organic ways in which he can partic-
ipate in controlling aims, methods, and materials of the school.*

—John Dewey (1916)

To have democracy, we must live it day by day.

—Mary Parker Follett (1940)

Democratic values have guided applied social reformers like Dewey and
Follett throughout the twentieth century in creating strategies for continuous improvement.

Dewey (1916) taught that society will be more productive as skills of participatory group work become common in our schools. He argued that group projects
should include you, your students, and your colleagues using problem-solving
methods together to solve the challenges you face in your school. He also envisioned
you and your students doing research in your own classroom.

Follett (1940) taught that individual potential will be released and contribute
more to continuous improvement when group problem solving occurs daily in our
society's organizations, including schools. She argued for a democratic alternative to
the top-down strategy for continuous improvement advocated by Frederick Taylor.

Whereas Taylor (1923), the creator of scientific management, taught that
managers should use time and motion research to impose, top down, the best way

to carry out industrial work, Follett argued that workers and managers should collaborate as participating partners to make their workplace more productive. Follett (1924 and 1940) wrote about empowering workers to do problem solving and action research on themselves in their own work settings.

Dewey and Follett envisioned social psychologists "giving away" their research methods to students, workers, and citizens at large.

THREE FACES OF CONTINUOUS IMPROVEMENT

Reflective practice, problem solving, and action research are the three faces of continuous improvement for individuals and organizations. Don Schön (1983 and 1987) taught that systematic reflection offers a fresh design for the teaching and learning professions. For your professional reflection to be systematic, Schön pointed to procedures like force field analysis, situation-target-path (STP) concepts, brainstorming and critical thinking, and self-confrontation. Reflection often precedes problem solving and action research, but it also can be an integral part of both. Dewey (1933) wrote that thinking and problem solving are the same, while Lewin (1948) saw action research as a means to solve problems.

In *The Handbook of Organization Development in Schools and Colleges* (1994, chap. 7), Philip Runkel and I laid out the steps of systematic problem solving. Our basic idea is that a problem is a discrepancy between a current situation and the goals for that situation, between a less than satisfactory present situation and more desirable goals for a future situation. The problem is being worked on as paths are found from the current situation to a future goal. We specified seven problem-solving steps as follows:

1. *Specify the Problem.* A problem is a discrepancy between your actual situation and your preferred goals. Ask two questions: What is wrong with the way things are now? and What would you like to accomplish that you are not accomplishing now? Your interest is why the present situation falls short of your goals.

2. *Assess the Situation With the Force Field Analysis.* Each situation has facilitating forces, which help us reach our goal, and restraining forces, which keep us from reaching our goal. The situation is in dynamic equilibrium when the opposing forces are equal in strength. The situation can be changed by adding facilitating forces and by subtracting restraining forces (for a classic example, see Coch and French 1948).

3. *Specify Multiple Solutions.* Brainstorm ways to increase the facilitating forces and to decrease the restraining forces. Be creative and inventive. Ronald Lippitt, my mentor in graduate school, told me that brainstorming should be exhilarating and inspirational and that he saw it as a key to planned change.

4. *Plan for Action.* Be critical and hard nosed in selecting only the brainstormed ideas you think are feasible and realistic. Through critical thinking, you create a plan for who will do what, when, and in what order.

5. *Anticipate Obstacles.* Think carefully about the barriers or hindrances that could arise as your plan unfolds. Use a second force field analysis on your

action plan. After you brainstorm forces that might stand in your way, modify your plan to take those hindering factors into consideration. That will give your plan a better chance of success.

6. *Take Action.* Implement your action plan. Reflect on the present, the here and now. Carry out the planned change.

7. *Evaluate.* Tally the strengths and weaknesses of your actions. With your evaluation, specify a new problem and recycle the seven steps of problem solving to engage in continuous improvement.

Figure 2.1 illustrates how a high school English teacher, Anne Hardy*, implemented the seven steps of problem solving in one class.

To achieve planned change, problem solving should be continual. As a mature educator, you believe that continuous self-improvement is your duty and responsibility.

ACTION RESEARCH: TWO TYPES OF SOCIAL SCIENTISTS

The third face of continuous improvement, the most complex and difficult, is action research. Called a "practical theorist" by his biographer, Alfred Marrow (1969), Kurt Lewin (1951) coined the term "action research." As the most influential social psychologist of the first half of the twentieth century, Lewin spawned a large legacy of two types of social psychologists: traditional researchers concerned with creating theory and testing hypotheses and action researchers concerned with solving problems and making changes.

Traditional researchers are epitomized by Leon Festinger, who did laboratory and field experiments to create theories about cognitive dissonance, reference groups, and social-comparison processes. Action researchers are epitomized by Ronald Lippitt, who did naturalistic field studies to create techniques of planned change, problem solving, group dynamics training, and school development. Both Festinger and Lippitt used Lewin's ideas to plan their own research. Festinger was one of my teachers; Lippitt was my mentor.

Lewin taught that both types of social psychologists make significant contributions to a better world. He envisioned researchers like Festinger and Lippitt in a complementary exchange and hoped that traditional and action researchers would exchange insights and wisdom. Lewin told his students often, "There is nothing so practical as a good theory" (Marrow 1969).

DIFFERENCES BETWEEN ACTION RESEARCH AND TRADITIONAL RESEARCH

In action research, you study your own situation to improve the quality of processes and results within it. By using research methods with your students on your practices, you are doing what will improve your practice continuously. Reading

---

* The name has been changed.

Figure 2.1   An Example of Problem Solving

1. Specify the Problem

   Anne Hardy, a high school English teacher, thinks that over half of the students do not like to write and do not write well. The target is that all students will like to write and be able to do so reasonably well.

2. Assess the Situation with the Force Field Analysis

Facilitating Forces	**Restraining Forces**
Some popular students like to write and can write reasonably well.	Many students spend a lot of time watching TV and do not read much.
I am quite interested in writing and have recently taken two workshops on writing.	I feel unsure about how to change students' attitudes toward writing.
The principal strongly supports my wish that the students write better.	Some of my colleagues do not allocate much time to teaching writing in their classes.
Many parents support my objective of improving students' attitudes and performance in writing.	Only a few students have computers at home.

3. Specify Multiple Solutions
   - Assign students to write about what they watch on TV.
   - Encourage students to take notes on the underlying messages on TV.
   - Seek ways to establish partnerships between students who like to write well and those who don't.
   - Talk with a few colleagues about a small project on writing with our students.
   - See if the principal will help me inspire the students about writing.
   - Check on whether a business organization will donate old computers to my class.

4. Plan for Action
   - **Next week:** Announce to the class that I want to test a new way to teach writing. It will involve writing about TV programs, much like a newspaper reporter does. During class, we will discuss the TV programs we watch, and each student will choose one or two to write about.
   - **The week after:** Invite the principal to work on writing with my class, talk with colleagues about a collaborative writing project, and call a few businesses about the availability of computers.
   - **The week after that:** Try to build partnerships between students to facilitate their attitudes toward and achievement in writing.

5. Anticipate Obstacles
   - A few of the good writers do not watch a lot of TV. (I might have to include movies seen at the theater along with TV in the first assignment.)
   - The principal might not have the time to help me. (I should consider getting a few volunteer tutors from the community.)
   - Calling will take a lot of time. (I might see if the school site council will take on that job.)
   - The students won't know how to work as partners. (I will do some training on giving and receiving feedback.)

6. Take Action
   - Implement the action plan.

7. Evaluate.
   - Give the same test to all students.
   - Talk with four students who have had difficulty with writing and two students who are good writers.
   - Ask the principal or tutors to watch for student involvement in writing.

Figure 2.2   Traditional Research

A social studies teacher must write a field study to earn a master's degree. He is required to state a research question, review what the research literature says about the question, and collect data in schools other than his own to answer the question. His research question is: Do only children and firstborns, compared to later borns, assume more leadership positions in the student government? His literature review reveals a mixed case, with a tendency for firstborns (but not only children) to take on student leadership positions more often than later borns. The teacher prepares a questionnaire to measure birth order and involvement in student government. He collects data from students at ten high schools in a neighboring county. He writes up the results, along with the literature review, research methods, data analysis, and conclusion. In the conclusion, he must return to the literature review to show how his study adds to the accumulating literature on the subject. His paper is read by his wife and a colleague and approved by two professors. One professor has encouraged him to try to get it published in the journal *Child Development.*

Figure 2.3   Action Research

A social studies teacher joins a network of teachers doing action research. She is expected to choose a problem in her own classroom or school. She focuses on her school, because as a faculty adviser, she sees a problem with the student council. She notes that over the last three years, fewer students have been volunteering to serve on the council and that more of those volunteers have been dropping out after only a couple of meetings. She decides to study all the students' perceptions and attitudes about the council with a questionnaire. She gets help with the questionnaire from teachers in the network. She collects and analyzes data, distributes results to students, faculty, and the administration, and works with an action research team of council and faculty members to brainstorm ways to improve council functioning. She announces new practices at a faculty meeting and a student assembly and works with the team to implement them. Later, team members interview new council members to see how the new practices are going. At the end of the school year, council members interview a sample of students and faculty.

traditional research can give you ideas and insights, but it usually will not connect directly with your situation. Much traditional research is carried out with the research community in mind; the results are published in scientific journals that are read by other traditional researchers. Action research, in contrast, is done by you to help you and your students and often will not be published, although more and more action research is being published nowadays.

Traditional research is often carried out by disinterested (objective) scientists, usually with concern for secrecy expressed as the principle of objectivity and a wish to establish generalized truths, often without immediate payoffs for research subjects. In action research, you remove the traditional gap between scientist and research subject because you are both "scientist" and a "subject" of research.

Traditional researchers look at what their subjects do and try not to become personally involved with them. Action researchers look at what they themselves are or should be doing, reflect on what they are thinking and feeling, and seek creative ways to improve how they are behaving. In other words, you conduct action research to improve your practices and the lives of your students. Study the cases in Figures 2.2 and 2.3 for actual examples of two types of research.

I do not want to pit traditional and action research against each other. I want to be clear about their differences, not pose a polemic. A good synthesis of traditional research can greatly benefit action researchers. As we see later, good traditional research is very useful when you search for knowledge or methods to use in your

Figure 2.4   Differences and Similarities Between Two Kinds of Research

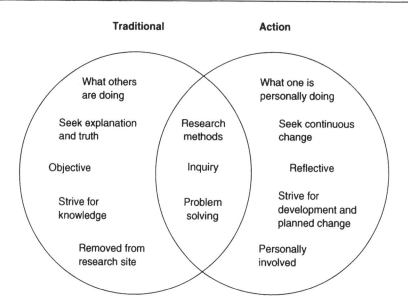

action research. You should make use of reviews and meta-analyses of traditional research and read traditional research to check out research methods you will use in your action research. Figure 2.4 shows the differences and similarities between traditional and action research. Note the area of overlap.

I see four core differences that stand out in how social psychologists of Lewin's legacy might have compared traditional with action research. They are summarized in Figure 2.5.

AN EXAMPLE OF ACTION RESEARCH

Figure 2.1 presented an example of problem solving in which Anne Hardy, a high school English teacher, sought to improve the writing performance of her students. Now look at how Robert Hess* (1996), another high school English teacher in a different school, did action research on student writing in a class of tenth graders.

Hess simultaneously served as developer, teacher, data collector, and data analyst. He was sole initiator, detector, and judge. Like Anne Hardy, Hess's objective was to improve his writing instruction.

Hess's writer's workshop, which he wrote about in a graduate class, offers students a choice in what and how they write and emphasizes process more than product. Hess, as teacher, acts like a counselor, moving from student to student for one-on-one help. Students work together in pairs to help each other write better.

Hess began his action research with three assumptions about the development of a writing program new to him. He assumed that (1) student-created writing portfolios (collections of personal writing) would be an important component of a high-quality writing curriculum, (2) his writer's workshop would work better than

---

*Thanks to Robert Hess for access to his action research project on the use of writing portfolios and their effect on motivating students to write.

Figure 2.5   Four Core Differences Between Action and Traditional Researchers

Improvement vs. Explanation	Development vs. Knowledge	Perspectives vs. Experimentation	Local vs. Universal
Action researchers seek a shared understanding of how those who work together affect one another. They are concerned with intervention for continuous improvement.	*Action researchers* wish to foster development and self-renewal of their own group or organization. They are concerned with planned change.	*Action researchers* strive to reach beyond their own limited points of view by collecting data on multiple perspectives of significant others. They are concerned with obtaining trustworthy information from the right people.	*Action researchers* work by themselves or engage colleagues in self-study and problem solving to increase local effectiveness. They are concerned with building tentative theories to guide future steps in the change and improvement process.
Traditional researchers seek to explain how social relations function, why people influence one another, and what characterizes an effective group or organization. They are concerned with explanation and truth.	*Traditional researchers* seek to build a body of knowledge about social relations that grow over time. They are concerned with accumulation of knowledge.	*Traditional researchers* strive to move outside their subjective realities by collecting data in controlled experiments or field studies. They are concerned with obtaining objective data from a representative sample.	*Traditional researchers* engage other researchers worldwide in studies to build universal theory. They are concerned with establishing generalized principles.

his traditional method of direct instruction, and (3) girls and boys would not differ in how they think and feel about their personal writing. His action research caused Hess to question seriously his second and third assumptions.

Hess designed his action research to last 12 weeks. He spent Weeks 1 to 6 doing traditional, direct instruction; he spent Weeks 7 to 12 doing writer's workshop. Hess collected informal observations during all 12 weeks. He also collected data with structured questionnaires three times: before he started teaching this class, after 6 weeks, and after 12 weeks.

Hess taught writing to five other classes of ninth graders at the same time. His understanding of the strengths and weaknesses of writer's workshop were enhanced by his other teaching experiences. He could not help but compare what occurred in the five ninth-grade classes with what took place in the "experimental" tenth-grade class. His experience surprised him.

Hess found that his writer's workshop, more that his direct instruction method, helped students develop favorable attitudes toward writing and build their self-confidence as writers. The writer's workshop, however, did not achieve what Hess had hoped for in students' high-quality writing.

In writer's workshop, students chose to write personal narratives or fragments of poems. Very few tried to write persuasive essays; even fewer wrote expository essays or research papers. In contrast, Hess observed that when he assigned his ninth graders persuasive or expository essays, many did take risks with their writing, reducing some of their reluctance to broaden the kinds of writing they would try. Hess concluded that while his writer's workshop was a positive experience for the tenth graders, his traditional procedures helped ninth graders learn to write better.

Although he did not expect it, Hess found too that girls and boys differed in the questionnaire results. Girls enjoyed writing more than boys and believed more than boys that they could write well. Even so, the girls lacked pride in the quality of their written products. The boys were just as proud, if not prouder than the girls, of their written products. His "blind assessments" of the students' writing portfolios in his writer's workshop led Hess to conclude that girls, for the most part, were better writers than boys.

Hess told me he benefited from this action research. The data helped him grow in perspective and become more mature about thinking through his teaching strategies. He decided that his next go-round with writing instruction would entail a new integration and synthesis of writer's workshop and direct instruction. He also intended to become more sensitive to how girls and boys approach writing and to focus future action research on differentiated instruction in writing for girls and boys.

PROCESSES OF CONTINUOUS IMPROVEMENT

Note the equilateral triangle in Figure 2.6. The three faces are respectively Reflective Practice, Problem Solving, and Action Research. The name of that triangle is Continuous Improvement. Use well-planned reflection and problem solving to fix your mind on topics for your action research, and as you do action research, use systematic reflection and problem solving to enhance your results. Chapters 3 through 8 teach you how to do action research.

Figure 2.6   Continuous Improvement

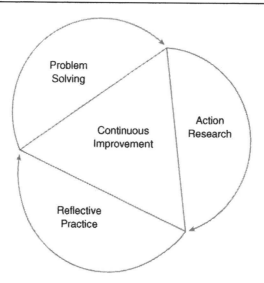

✤ Reflections

Reflect on Chapter 2 by answering the following questions:

1. Have you been engaged in formal problem solving? Describe what happened.

2. What do you think about the differences between traditional research and action research?

3. Have you been involved in a traditional research project? Describe what happened.

4. Have you been involved in an action research project? Describe what happened.

5. How might traditional research benefit you, your students, and your school?

6. How might action research benefit you, your students, and your school?

Seven Problem-Solving Steps

Think of a professional problem you face. Write a few sentences for each of the seven steps.

1. Specify the problem (focus on gaps between *S* and *T*).

2. Assess the situation with the force field analysis (use critical thinking).

3. Specify multiple solutions (use brainstorming).

4. Plan for action (use critical thinking).

5. Anticipate obstacles (reflect on the future).

6. Take action (reflect on the present).

7. Evaluate (reflect on the past).

Action Research

Definitions, Models, Steps, and Phases

The action of action research . . . implies change in people's lives and therefore in the system in which they live.

—J. McNiff and J. Whitehead (2000)

Action research is . . . conducted by . . . the people empowered to take action . . . for the purpose of improving their future action.

—Richard Sagor (2005)

Change is where action research leads. McNiff and Whitehead (2000) tell why I have added the words *for change* to the title of this book, and Sagor (2005) adds that local people bring about change through action research.

CONTEMPORARY NEED FOR ACTION RESEARCH

Increasing public pressure for school change continues unabated year after year. Throughout my career as a social psychologist (over 45 years), the mass media have criticized schools for our students' low achievement in language, history, math, and science. Parents have expressed concern for their children's low opportunity for college success because of inadequate preparation in K–12 schools. Even after 20 years of planned change sponsored by Theodore Sizer's (1984, 1992) Coalition of Essential Schools, the American public still yearns for better senior high schools. Demands for innovative charter schools have been expressed nationwide during the last ten years.

Public schools also have come under fire from business leaders for failing to prepare young people adequately in the job-related skills of group planning, cooperative teamwork, and collective problem solving. The ever-blossoming information industry of the twenty-first century places a premium on young adults' capabilities to adapt to unpredictable challenges in a changing workplace and a cyberspace world. Knowing how to learn new things, creating brand-new solutions to problems, and working cooperatively with others in new circumstances have become as important as learning academic subject matter.

Sizer (1992) wrote, "Good schools are organic places, always in constructive and sensitive motion" (p. 142). My view is that schools will not get into constructive and sensitive motion until administrators, teachers, and students work together to create conditions in which learning how to learn, stretching to be creative, and doing cooperative projects become regular practices. Nor will schools sustain organic growth without local teams asking (1) Why are we doing what we are doing? (2) What are we doing that is effective or ineffective? (3) Where do we want to go? and (4) How do we plan to get there? To put it in the words of Chapter 2: reflection, problem solving, and action research should make up a part of a school's repertoire for the school to become organic.

Start with yourself, your own class. What do you want the social-emotional climate of your class to be? What student attitudes are most important to you? What student outcomes are most significant to you? What about your school's organizational climate? Do you and your colleagues talk about it? What teachers' attitudes are most important to you? What school outcomes are most significant to you? Delve into answers to questions like those to find a focus for action research.

DEFINITIONS OF ACTION RESEARCH

Action research entails studying your own situation to change the quality of processes and results within it. To do action research is to empower yourself to study your actions so that your future actions will be more effective. It also aims to improve your professional judgments and to give you insight into how better to achieve your educational goals. Through action research, you can convert current practices into better procedures, better instructional strategies, and better curriculum. Remember too that action research is a continuous and cyclical professional activity that is integrated into your regular practice. Figure 3.1 offers a list of seven similes or metaphors to action research. Can you think of some others?

Jean McNiff (1997), a secondary school administrator and author of several books on action research, exhorts you to use action research to change your life and the system in which you live. She writes about two changes that should preoccupy your thinking as a professional. The first focuses on your personal theories for how your students learn. The second focuses on effects your actual practices have on your students. She argues that action research invites you to test your personal theories and practices about student learning by gathering data to convince yourself that your current theories and practices should be changed.

Use action research to understand how significant others, such as your students, parents, or colleagues, see you and how they are affected by you. Undertake action research to grow beyond your solitary dialogues to engage significant others in

Figure 3.1   Action Research Is Like . . .

- Acting as a detective to uncover clues about the effects of one's work
- Spying on oneself to get the scoop about one's own actions
- Watching a movie of oneself or one's own group in action
- Reading critics' reviews on the morning after opening night
- Collecting Nielsen ratings on one's television program
- Eavesdropping on people's conversations as they leave a play one has presented
- Listening to judges' ratings during a gymnastics competition

Try brainstorming other appropriate similes or metaphors to action research.

"external conversations" about how you and others affect them. Use action research to find out how you should practice differently to be more effective.

Action research is planned inquiry, a deliberate search for information, perspectives, or knowledge. It consists of both self-reflective inquiry, which is internal and subjective, and inquiry-oriented practice, which is external and data based. Action research is a formal investigation into yourself or into your own social system.

Action research consists of planned, continuous, and systematic procedures for learning about your professional practice and for trying out alternative practices to improve outcomes. It unfolds through a spiral of cycles: reflecting, planning, acting, data collecting, analyzing, replanning, acting, data collecting, reflecting; or reflecting, data collecting, analyzing, reflecting, planning, acting, data collecting, and so on.

As an alternative to traditional research, action research is

- *Practical.* Insights that you get from data lead to practical changes in your classroom or in your school during and immediately after the inquiry (e.g., class climate, student achievement, and staff morale can be improved).
- *Participative.* As action researchers, you and your students or you and your colleagues collect data about a real issue in your shared situation. You are not outside, disinterested experts conducting inquiries on research subjects (e.g., action researchers are teachers, students, and administrators in collaboration or cooperation).
- *Empowering.* All of you together can influence and contribute equally to the research (e.g., teachers with students or administrators with teachers cooperate as equals in the research process).
- *Interpretive.* Social realities of your situation are determined collaboratively by pooling participants' perceptions and attitudes during the inquiry (e.g., you and your students share your perceptions and attitudes with one another).
- *Tentative.* Inquiries do not result in your coming up with right or wrong answers but rather with tentative solutions based on participants' diverse views (e.g., you and your colleagues decide to try out new meeting procedures for three months).
- *Critical.* You and other participants not only search for practical improvements in your situation, but you also act as self-critical change agents (e.g., teachers ask students for feedback about the strengths and weaknesses of their teaching methods).

ACTION RESEARCH AND GROUP DYNAMICS

Even though you are responsible for initiating action research in your own class, school, or district, you never do action research alone. Action research is collaborative, participatory, and reciprocal. As a teacher, you enlist your students' coparticipation to plan and execute research. As a principal, you engage your faculty; as a superintendent, your staff or board. Together, teacher and students, principal and faculty, or superintendent, staff, or school board, carry out action research as partners.

In contrast to the collaborative norms of action research, traditional research is usually carried out via role relationships of hierarchical power between experts and their subjects. Note the label *subjects.* The researchers' methods and the evolving relationship as the design unfolds put traditional researchers in an authority role over their subjects. The researcher unilaterally decides what to investigate, who and what to study and for how long, what instructions to give to the subjects, and what to do with the data after they are analyzed. At the end of a traditional research project, only researchers receive recognition for the research. Researchers often publish results in a scientific journal, not immediately accessible to the subjects.

Traditional researchers prepare hypotheses, then collect data to test them. An appropriate metaphor is that of a detective who seeks to identify a criminal. The detective's data lead toward a definite conclusion, the identity of the criminal. That style of scientific research works most effectively when clear answers exist to a research hypothesis. Action research is tentative and critical; it is less definite than traditional research.

Typically, the traditional researcher focuses on the research hypothesis, not on the actual people who are being studied. They are "subjects"; they are not whole persons. The simile that comes to my mind is that traditional researchers are like kings associating with their subjects, the people who make up their kingdom. The king does not care who does what for him so long as what he wants done gets done.

At their best, traditional researchers are studious managers or curious visitors. In contrast, action researchers are democratic leaders or moral participants. Whether it is done in a class, a school, or a district, freedom and equality are necessary conditions of action research. William Foote Whyte (1991), an expert on action research in agriculture, business, and public administration, called it "participatory action research"; Richard Sagor (2005) called it "collaborative action research." Figure 3.2 lists some possible action research teams.

Cooperative group work to study ourselves is a basic process of action research. That is true even when you initiate and coordinate your own action research in your own classroom. Even as an individual teacher or as a lone administrator, you must engage others in the action research process. Nowadays, a good deal of action research is not carried out by individual teachers working alone with their students. It is often organized from the start as a group effort or a team project, in subsystems with such names as site councils, climate committees, evaluation groups, planning task forces, or leadership teams.

Because democratic participation and egalitarian cooperation are essential to action research, you must have more than knowledge about research methods to do it well. You should also be capable of executing group-dynamics skills such as communication techniques, joint goal-setting methods, group problem-solving sequences, and consensual decision-making procedures. Action research calls for

Figure 3.2   Action Research Teams

Action research topics on the left are followed by possible research teams on the right.

Action Research	Implemented by
To improve classroom social-emotional climate	Students and students
	Teacher and students
	Teacher and parents
	Teacher, students, and parents
To evaluate a new curriculum	Teachers and teachers
	Teachers and students
	Teachers and parents
	Teachers and curriculum specialists
To change report cards	Administrators and teachers
	Administrators, teachers, and students
	Administrators, teachers, and staff members
	Administrators, teachers, staff members, and parents
To study sexual harassment	District office personnel and school administrators
	District office personnel, school administrators, and teachers
	District office personnel, school administrators, teachers, and students
	District office personnel, school administrators, teachers, students, parents, and staff members

cooperative group dynamics through which you share data and jointly search for solutions to problems or for new ways to reach shared goals.

Effective action research is democracy in action, especially as the action research fosters group reflection, joint inquiry, shared debriefing, and cooperative action planning. Action research can help establish those schools that Sizer (1992) so aptly called "organic places, always in constructive and sensitive motion" (p. 142).

TWO MODELS OF ACTION RESEARCH

The two models of action research, proactive and responsive, differ primarily when data are collected and analyzed during the research cycle. In proactive action research, action precedes data collection. You act and then study the effects of your actions. In responsive action research, data are collected and analyzed before action is taken. You diagnose the situation or carry out a needs assessment before you take action. In both models, action and data collection are alternating events, which means that after start-up, both models are similar.

Proactive Action Research

In being proactive, you are inspired to try a new practice. Your inspiration might arise from your reflections on your past and future, your debriefings with your students or colleagues, or hopes and aspirations that came into your mind during an inservice workshop or college course. Often, your creative inspirations about a new practice will come as you think about how to tighten the coupling between your values and your practices. The steps of the proactive model are as follows:

1. List hopes and concerns for the new practice.
2. After a knowledge search, try a new practice, to have different effects on students and to bring about better outcomes.
3. Do a methods search to create research procedures; then collect data to track students' reactions and behavioral changes.
4. Check on what the data mean.
5. Reflect on alternative ways to behave.
6. Fine-tune the new practice or try a different new practice.

The sequence travels cyclically; return to Step 1.
See Figure 3.3 for examples of each step in proactive action research.

Responsive Action Research

In the responsive model, you collect diagnostic data before you try a new practice. Your decision to use it might arise out of your belief that your situation is unclear and it is your professional responsibility to understand your situation better before acting. You might also remember a time when a new action you took backfired because the students did not understand what you were trying to do. The steps of the responsive models are as follows:

1. After a methods search, collect data to diagnose the situation.
2. Analyze the data for themes and ideas for action.
3. Do a knowledge search, distribute the data, and announce changes that will be tried.
4. List hopes and concerns for the new practice.
5. Try the new practice, to have a different effect on students and to bring about better outcomes.
6. Collect data to evaluate the effects of the new practice.

The cycle should continue; return to Step 2.
See Figure 3.4 for examples of each step in responsive action research.

The Models Compared

The two models differ primarily at start-up. Once a continuous cycle is under way, they both call for revised action and new research, followed by more new action and more new research. Kurt Lewin told Ron Lippitt, "No research without action and no action without research" (personal communication).

Each model gains in power as it incorporates important aspects of the other. Both models list hopes and concerns before a new practice is tried, because the hopes and concerns must be considered before the new practice is launched. Also, the hopes become the outcomes that are measured to see if the new practice has been effective.

Figure 3.3   Steps of Proactive Action Research

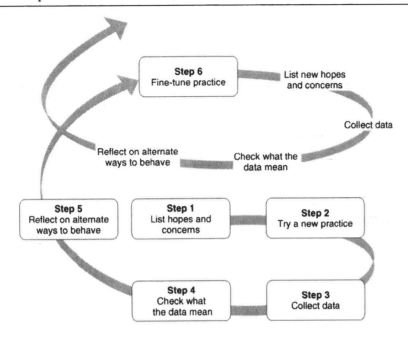

Steps	Examples

1. List hopes and concerns. Hopes are goals to strive toward. Concerns are obstacles to avoid or barriers to overcome.	Hopes:
	  a. Students will use cooperative learning effectively.
	  b. Students will work harder and make fewer mistakes.
	  c. Assessments will be meaningful and engaging to students.
	Concerns:
	  a. Students will not work hard and will hitchhike on their peers.
	  b. Students will resist new methods.
	  c. Students are so insecure that they will reject the new procedures.

2. Try a new practice to have a different effect on students or to bring about better outcomes.	a. A new way to prepare students to work in groups b. A new method to teach part of the curriculum c. A new procedure for students to assess their learning with portfolios
3. Collect data regularly to keep track of students' reactions and behavioral changes.	a. Teacher regularly has students fill out questionnaires and asks a committee of five students to observe group work. b. Teacher has a colleague observe the class and keep a journal. c. Teacher sends questionnaires to parents and interviews students.
4. Check on what the data mean.	a. Teacher holds discussions weekly with the class to analyze data on group work. b. Colleague-to-colleague exchanges occur weekly about the new method. c. A parent committee reviews the new assessment procedures.
5. Reflect on alternative ways to behave.	a. Teacher writes a solitary dialogue between his or her caring and confrontational selves. b. Teacher reflects in the past, present, and future about the new practice. c. Teacher finishes sentence stem: I prefer to motivate by evaluating their academic work by _____ _____
6. Fine-tune the practice. (The sequence has traveled full circle back to Step 1).	a. For the next group work, students work in pairs before creating larger groups. b. Teacher tries a few of his or her colleague's ideas to revise the new teaching method. c. Teacher prepares a brief explanation of portfolio assessment for parents.

Figure 3.4   Steps of Responsive Action Research

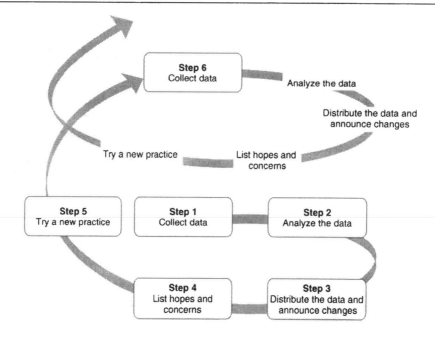

Steps	Examples
1. Collect data to diagnose the situation.	a. School-climate committee gets questionnaire data from staff members about the school's emotional climate. b. Site council members interview parents on the school's strengths and weaknesses. c. Administrative cabinet observes citizens at extracurricular programs.
2. Analyze the data for themes and ideas for action.	a. Committee notes a large gap between certified faculty and classified staff. b. Site council notes that parents are satisfied with math and science courses but dissatisfied with students' writing skills. c. Cabinet sees large numbers of citizens attend boys' sports events but too few attend girls' sports events.
3. Distribute the data to others and announce changes that will be tried.	a. School climate committee announces a workshop to improve communication between teachers and other staff. b. Site council announces a series of small group discussions with heterogeneous teacher groups. c. Administrative cabinet tells staff and PTA it will launch advertising to attract adults to girls' sports events.
4. List hopes and concerns.	Hopes: a. Enhance climate of staff. b. Upgrade students' writing skills. c. Increase parent attendance at girls' sports. Concerns: a. Teachers feel overworked. b. Some students are afraid to write. c. Most community members are more interested in boys' sports than girls' sports.
5. Try a practice to have a different effect on others.	a. School climate committee runs a four-hour workshop on "getting to know our colleagues better—it takes all working together to educate our youngsters." b. Site council runs teacher workshops on writing across the curriculum. c. The cabinet enlists 15 volunteers to run an advertising campaign for girls' sports events.
6. Collect data to check how others are reacting and collect data to diagnose the situation (the sequence has circled back to Step 1).	a. School climate committee watches to see that certified and classified staff become better acquainted and then collects questionnaire data to see if the communication gap between them has been reduced. b. Site council gives special encouragement to language teachers and assesses how well writing across the curriculum is going through interviews with a random sample of teachers. c. Administrative cabinet reinforces the 15 volunteers with telephone calls and makes structured, direct observations to measure citizens' participation at girls' sports events.

By taking the concerns into consideration, the new practice can be modified to increase its effectiveness.

Both models call for a knowledge search and a methods search. In the proactive model, the knowledge search comes early, because a new practice's success is based on the practice having been tried successfully in other settings. In the responsive model, the methods search comes early, because an accurate diagnosis of the situation is critical to the success of the project. The presence of both searches in both models reminds us of how important contributions of traditional research can be to the success of action research.

THREE PHASES OF ACTION RESEARCH

Three phases of action recur and recycle through all action research projects: initiation, detection, and judgment. Figure 3.5 illustrates when the phases occur in proactive and responsive action research. You collect data at each of these phases to understand what you are doing or to reflect on what you should do.

Initiation

At initiation, you reflect on the future and inquire about what actions you should

Figure 3.5 Phases of Action Research

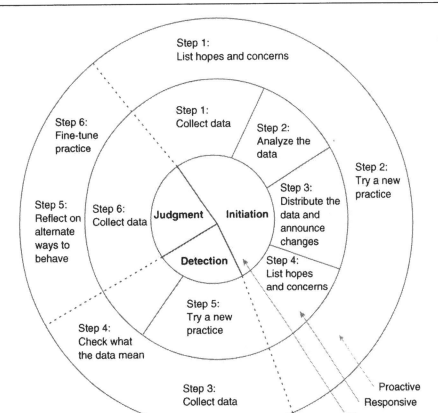

take first. Richard Sagor (2005) refers to this phase as "research for action." In proactive action research, action is initiated before data collection; therefore, research for action entails reflecting on past experiences, searching knowledge bases, and brainstorming with colleagues. In responsive action research, data collection precedes action; therefore, research for action entails collecting data through questionnaires, interviews, observations, and documents. Figure 3.6 lists some examples of initiation.

Detection

During detection, you monitor and adjust your actions from time to time. Detection requires reflection on the present, the here and now. Sagor (2005) calls this phase "research in action." It is similar to what Michael Scriven (1980) calls "formative evaluation" or what the Lewineans refer to as "process analysis" during training group sessions (Bradford, Gibb, and Benne 1964). Figure 3.7 lists some examples of detection.

Judgment

During judgment, you collect data on the results of your actions over the long haul (e.g., from month to month, semester to semester, and year to year) and on student outcomes. Sagor (2005) calls this phase "research of action." It is similar to Scriven's (1980) "summative evaluation," although in action research you execute judgment to see how well your new practices contributed to positive student outcomes. You do not necessarily do it for policy makers, for which the concept of summative evaluation has often been applied. Judgment entails reflection on the past; it is systematic inquiry into what has or has not been achieved with your new actions over a considerable time period.

Figure 3.6   Examples of Initiation

- Searching for and deciding on new curriculum materials
- Diagnosing abilities, attitudes, concepts, feelings, perceptions, and skills of students
- Assessing how comfortable, included, and secure girls and boys (or African Americans, European Americans, Hispanic Americans, and Native Americans) feel with one another
- Becoming acquainted with multiple parts of students' self-concepts
- Introducing an innovative teaching method

Figure 3.7   Examples of Detection

- Interviewing students about their initial reactions to the new curriculum materials
- Observing how students with different abilities, attitudes, concepts, feelings, perceptions, and skills react to different aspects of the class
- Looking for circumstances in which girls and boys (or African Americans, European Americans, Hispanic Americans, and Native Americans) feel involved in or left out of classroom activities
- Observing verbal and nonverbal indicators of high and low student self-esteem
- Collecting questionnaire data once a week on students' perceptions of the innovative teaching method

When collecting data on student outcomes, you seek to judge what Scriven (1980) called "merit and worth of results." To achieve merit, a result must have intrinsic value. Gold, for instance, has merit when you perceive it as beautiful and have favorable attitudes toward wearing it. For Scriven, the merit of a student outcome is measured by the psychological reactions of the students. In classroom action research, you might assess merit by gathering data about students' subjective responses, such as their perceptions, concepts, feelings, attitudes, and values.

To achieve worth, a result must have extrinsic value. Gold, for instance, has worth because it can be exchanged for money; thus you can say that gold is worth so many dollars an ounce. The worth of a student outcome is measured by students' performances and subsequent accomplishments. In classroom action research, you assess worth by gathering data on students' information, skill, and capability of carrying out particular actions. In contrast to a focus on attitudes, as when you judge merit, use achievement tests to measure worth. Test your students to see if they have knowledge, skill, or capability (e.g., students can read and comprehend what they have read, or students can solve math problems correctly). Figure 3.8 lists examples of judgment.

Research During Each Phase

Each phase of action research entails research. Initiation calls for either a data collection, as in the responsive model, or a knowledge search by reading or conferring, as in the proactive model. Detection calls for data collections to track how new actions are working. Judgment calls for data collections to assess results and to revise the actions so they will be more effective in reaching desired goals. Clearly, data collections distinguish action research from other types of professional development.

Figure 3.8   Examples of Judgment

Judging Merit	Judging Worth
Assessing students' attitudes toward different parts of the new curriculum materials	Testing students' recall and understanding of high points in the new curriculum materials
Measuring how students with different abilities, attitudes, concepts, feelings, perceptions, and skills value different aspects of the class	Observing how much students with different abilities, attitudes, concepts, feelings, perceptions, and skills stick with the tasks of different aspects of classroom work
Assessing girls' and boys' (or African Americans', European Americans', Hispanic Americans', and Native Americans') feelings of acceptance or alienation toward different classroom activities	Observing how often girls and boys (or African Americans, European Americans, Hispanic Americans, and Native Americans) perform task and social-emotional roles during cooperative group projects
Measuring students' academic self-esteem in relation to language arts, science, math, social studies, etc.	Testing students' understanding of academic subjects, such as language arts, science, math, social studies
Assessing students' attitudes toward different aspects of the new teaching method	Testing how well students apply what they have learned from a new teaching method to the solution of a community problem

Reflections

Reflect on Chapter 3 by answering the following questions:

1. Do you see issues in your current situation for which you might carry out action research?

2. If you were to do proactive action research, on what new practices might you focus?

3. If you were to do responsive action research, how might you collect diagnostic data?

4. Which of the two models do you prefer for your current situation? Explain why.

5. Do you see reflection, problem solving, and action research as the three faces of continuous improvement? Why or why not?

✿ Proactive Action Research

To expand your understanding of this model, brainstorm examples for each of the following:

1. Hopes and concerns that you might have

2. New practices that might interest you

3. Data collection methods that you might use

4. Procedures you might use to check out what the data mean

5. Strategies you might use to find alternative ways to behave

6. Strategies you might use to fine-tune the new practice

✽ Responsive Action Research

To expand your understanding of this model, brainstorm examples for each of the following:

1. Research methods you might use to diagnose your situation

2. Strategies you might use to analyze the data to find themes

3. Strategies you might use to feed the data back to announce changes

4. Hopes and concerns you might have

5. New practices you might want to try

6. Ways you might go about evaluating your new practices

4

Research Methods

Procedures, Instruments,
Special Issues,
and Ethics

Listen to the voice of the students. They are not afraid to talk about what actually happens in school.

—Herbert Kohl (1969)

In the last analysis, the worth of educational research is judged by its contributions to the improvement of educational practice.

—Stephen Corey (1953)

Herbert Kohl (1969), a high school drama teacher and author of *The Open Classroom*, reminds us that students communicate openly with receptive teachers about what happens in class and that students can be trusted to speak honestly and give valid data about their school experiences.

Stephen Corey (1953), a pioneer in action research to improve school practices, emphasizes that the value of any research, traditional or action, lies in how much it facilitates improved educational practice.

Although traditional and action research differ in purposes, they overlap in the research methods they employ. Both use methods to obtain data that follow three procedures: (1) asking questions, (2) observing behaviors, and (3) using existing data gathered by someone else.

Social researchers ask questions by using questionnaires and interviews or, in educational research, by using academic tests. They observe behaviors with an objective plan and systematic procedure. They use existing data in the form of public documents, census information, and school records.

The three procedures result in raw data that are coded for analysis by reducing them to categories or numbers. Data coded into categories are qualitative. Qualitative data describe characteristics of people or events according to nominal categories that cannot be scaled into equal intervals. Data coded into numbers are quantitative. Quantitative data describe amounts of characteristics of people or events, according to cardinal numbers that can be arranged into equal intervals.

DATA COLLECTION IN ACTION RESEARCH

Formal data collection distinguishes action research from reflection and problem solving. Data collection is at the center of proactive action research; it starts responsive action research. Data collection takes place in every phase of action research. Effective action research requires planned procedures and instruments for gathering data. The primary instruments are questionnaires, interview formats, observation systems, academic tests, and public or private documents. By private documents, I refer to personal journals or diaries.

Questionnaires

At times called inventories, opinionnaires, or surveys, questionnaires are printed lists of interrogative or declarative statements that individuals respond to in writing. They normally respond to questionnaires privately and in anonymity, but groups do respond to questionnaires using discussion and polling. Questionnaires can ask for facts, feelings, thoughts, or behaviors; they can be simple or complex; they can be open ended or have rating scales.

Factual Questionnaires

Factual questionnaires have items of information about which respondents have knowledge. The researcher described in Figure 2.2 used birth order as an independent variable in his traditional research. He measured it by using a factual questionnaire:

In your nuclear family, are you? (check one)

___ An only child

___ A firstborn

___ A second born

___ A third or later born

How many sisters do you have? _____

(print the number)

How many brothers do you have? _____

(print the number)

What is your sex?   M   F

(circle one)

He also used factual questions to measure the dependent variable: involvement in student government:

Think about the students in your school who take part in its student government.

Have you been or are you now a member of your school's student government?	Yes	No
		(circle one)

If yes, for how many years have you been in student government? (check one)

____ less than one year

____ one year or more, but less than two

____ two years or more, but less than three

____ three years or more

If yes, have you been or are you now an officer?	Yes	No
		(circle one)

If yes, print your officer titles below:

_____

_____

_____

Standardized Tests: Special Factual Questionnaires

Standardized tests can determine the worth of a new practice. They were particularly valued as a tool to ensure educators' accountability under the No Child Left Behind Act. Like factual questionnaires, they present items about which students should have knowledge; students write their answers privately but almost never in anonymity. Although academic testing could be done with interviews and observations (as it was when I taught in Belgium), American standardized tests typically are paper-and-pencil questionnaires. Most districts maintain a collection of standardized tests. Another source is the latest edition of *The Mental Measurements Yearbook* (Spies and Plake 2005) or Google or Yahoo! on the Internet.

Questionnaires About Feelings

Questionnaires about feelings have items of information about which respondents hold attitudes. An example of an open-ended attitudinal item is presented in Figure 6.4, How I Feel About Others in My Class. In a procedure known as sociometric inquiry, each respondent gets a class list on which every student's name is printed next to a number. Then an open-ended question is asked: "Which three students in this class do you like the most?" The student responds: "The three I like most are . . ." and then lists the students' numbers from the class list.

Another procedure to measure feelings is a structured rating scale, such as the Likert scale (pronounced Lick-urt). The Likert scale has five points: strongly agree

(SA), agree (A), neutral (N), disagree (D), and strongly disagree (SD). The questionnaire presents declarative statements, each accompanied by a Likert scale. For example:

(Circle one for each item)

I like reading books	SA	A	N	D	SD
I like math	SA	A	N	D	SD
I like art projects	SA	A	N	D	SD
I like writing stories	SA	A	N	D	SD

Questionnaires About Thoughts

One way to measure students' thoughts about school is for them to write open-ended responses in journals. During the last 30 minutes on the last day of the week, for example, students write their thoughts about the high and low points of the week in their journals.

Another open-ended strategy for measuring students' thoughts is the sentence-completion questionnaire. For example:

I learn best when _____.

Homework is _____.

Some of the best things about this class are _____.

Learning out of books is _____.

To measure students' thoughts with more structure, try a 5-point frequency rating scale: 5 = frequently, 4 = often, 3 = sometimes, 2 = seldom, and 1 = infrequently. Example items are as follows:

(Circle one)

I think about my schoolwork	5	4	3	2	1
I think about afterschool activities	5	4	3	2	1
I think about my homework	5	4	3	2	1
I think about weekends	5	4	3	2	1

Questionnaires About Behaviors

To measure students' perceptions of their own behaviors, try a 6-point frequency rating scale: 6 = six or more times a week, 5 = five times a week, 4 = four times a week, 3 = three times a week, 2 = two times a week, and 1 = one time or zero per week. Example items are as follows:

(Circle one)

I do homework	6	5	4	3	2	1
I read books	6	5	4	3	2	1

I play sports	6	5	4	3	2	1
I work on the computer	6	5	4	3	2	1
I work on math	6	5	4	3	2	1

To measure students' perceptions of your teaching, Figure 5.1, Our Teacher, in Chapter 5 offers a structure to measure a combination of students' perceptions and feelings about your behaviors. For each item, your students express their preferences for your behavior by checking one rating: much more, a little more, the same, a little less, or much less.

Tips on Making Questionnaires

Integrate the use of questionnaires into your regular instruction. Use them to enhance student involvement in learning.

You can create simple open-ended questionnaires quickly. The simplest way is to have students use a blank index card or piece of paper with a plus sign on top of one side and a minus sign on top of the other. Ask students to list helpful or supportive things about an aspect of your teaching on the plus side and to list unhelpful or non-supportive things about the same teaching aspect on the minus side. Do not give long explanations for the simple questionnaire; most students will complete them quickly. Answers to simple open-ended questions often uncover responses that surprise you. Anonymous data can supply you with rich and colorful quotations for later feedback discussions and student problem solving.

Consider structuring open-ended questionnaires to ensure that your students reveal sufficient data for analysis and discussion. Ask students to write three things about the class that help them learn and three things about the class that hinder their learning. Assigning specific numbers of things (e.g., three and three) will enhance your chances of obtaining a variety of answers, a few unexpected thoughts, and some powerful quotes worth subsequent discussion. If every student is prodded to give six answers, with 25 students you could get 150 answers for analysis, quantitative feedback, and class discussion. Furthermore, by adding instructions to your data collection, you are stimulating your students to think seriously and deeply about their answers and to move them beyond superficial clichés.

However easy open-ended questions are for your tailored action research, they have disadvantages. You could find that some answers are ambiguous, that different words have the same meaning, or that the same word has different meanings. Also, an analysis of the multiple answers could take time.

Most disadvantages of open-ended questionnaires can be reduced by using rating scales. As I demonstrated in the questionnaires about facts, feelings, thoughts, and behaviors, simple statements with rating scales can effectively measure students' reactions, and they can be answered and tallied quickly. You also will find it easier with rating scales to portray data clearly in tables and figures for feedback and problem solving.

You can present structured questionnaires with rating scales in several ways. Ask students to put a check or an X by specific items that apply to them, as in measuring students' birth order. Or give students the Likert scale to indicate whether they (SA) strongly agree, (A) agree, (N) feel neutral, (D) disagree, or (SD) strongly disagree. For example, if you have been trying cooperative group projects in writing, have your students respond to

(Circle one)

I think working cooperatively in groups
has helped me become a better writer.   SA   A   N   D   SD

or simply,

(Circle one)

I like how we use cooperative groups
to learn to write better.   SA   A   N   D   SD

You can also use the semantic differential, a classic procedure originated by psychologists Osgood, Suci, and Tannenbaum (1957). Have students circle a point on a rating scale with opposite-meaning adjectives at either end, such as helpful-unhelpful, interesting-not interesting, fun-not fun. For example,

Working on writing in cooperative groups is *(circle one number for every item)*

1. Helpful _____ _____ _____ _____ _____ Unhelpful
          +2   +1   0   −1   −2

2. Interesting _____ _____ _____ _____ _____ Not interesting
             +2   +1   0   −1   −2

3. Fun _____ _____ _____ _____ _____ Not fun
      +2   +1   0   −1   −2

Another similar procedure, with an even-numbered scale to avoid neutral responses, is the following:

I think working cooperatively in groups has helped me become a better writer.

(Circle one number)

Agree   6   5   4   3   2   1   Disagree

or

I like how we use cooperative groups to learn how to write better.

(Circle one number)

Always   6   5   4   3   2   1   Never

As you compose statements, remember to focus on a single issue in each one, such as "cooperative group projects in writing." Note that if you ask students in one statement to respond to "cooperative group projects in writing and social studies," students with contrasting attitudes toward writing and social studies would circle "neutral" on a Likert scale or a 3 or 4 on a 6-point scale to show how their two different attitudes combine. Seek too to keep rating scales consistent throughout each questionnaire. Do not use Likert scales, semantic differentials, and frequency scales in the same questionnaire. Create different questionnaires for each, or clearly different sections for each in the same questionnaire.

Add open-ended questions to a structured questionnaire to obtain richer data. For example, after statements with rating scales about cooperative groups, add, "In the open space, please write three things you want to stay the same in our cooperative writing groups and three things you would like changed."

Questionnaires are most useful to

- Announce the start of a responsive action research project
- Understand students' subjective states, their perceptions, ideas, feelings, cognitions, attitudes, and values
- Quantify students' responses
- Have all students respond to the same statements at the same time
- Collect a lot of data in a short time
- Allow students to be anonymous

Figure 4.1 highlights the advantages versus the disadvantages of questionnaires.

Interviews

Interviews are oral conversations; interviewers pose questions to interviewees. They are with individuals, one-on-one, or focus groups, in which a small face-to-face group is asked to discuss specific topics. Interviews vary in how informal or formal they are. Often, formal interviews are audio or video recorded. Four interview procedures follow.

One-on-One Informal Interviews

Integrate informal interviews with students into your normal, daily teaching; do not add them to an already busy duty schedule.

Figure 4.1   Advantages vs. Disadvantages of Questionnaires

Advantages	Disadvantages
Open-ended questions can be created easily and quickly.	Open-ended responses can be ambiguous.
Respondents can complete them quickly.	Analysis of open-ended responses takes time.
Open-ended responses offer rich quotations that are useful for data feedback.	If questions with rating scales include two or more ideas, the results will be unclear.
The chance of learning unexpected things is improved by asking for a few responses to the same question.	The data collector cannot ask respondents to clarify their answers.
Questions with rating scales can be scored quickly, and results can be clearly presented in graphic tables and figures.	The data collector has little opportunity to establish trust and rapport with the respondents.

In the informal interview, seek relaxed and spontaneous conversations with individual students to uncover their perceptions, thoughts, and attitudes. Do not record informal conversations; rather, make mental notes and later write summaries of students' responses in your journal. Ask only a few questions: "What did you like about the cooperative group work this morning?" "I see! Anything else?" "How would you like to change the way we do the cooperative work?" "Yes. Tell me more!"

In these interviews, ask open-ended questions. Follow them with silence, wait time, and short probes to facilitate additional conversation. Smile a lot but talk little; listen intently with your ears and eyes. Seek empathy. Paraphrase the students' answers, but briefly. Initiate informal interviews before class, in hallways while passing, at recess, at lunch, or after school. Seek to interview informally during interstices of school life, during those moments between and around formal instruction.

Focus Group Informal Interviews

Also casual and spontaneous, chat with a natural group of peers about their views of an event or project. You might ask, "What do you guys think about the cooperative group work we did this morning?" "Anyone else feel that way?" "Other ideas?" "How many agree with that?" With your relaxed questioning, try to get a count of how many group members felt one way or another. Do focus group informal interviews standing with the group after class, when you and the group happen to be in the same place in school, or during lunch at a cafeteria table.

One-on-One Formal Interviews

In the formal interview, state that action research is under way and that you wish to collect data to improve how the class operates. Develop a logical list of unambiguous questions and try them out on a few others before asking them of students in action research. Checking out your questions is "pilot testing"; it's a dry run in which you have opportunities to polish questions and rehearse in what order to ask them.

Start formal interviews with broad, open-ended questions: "Tell me how you feel about the class," and proceed, in a funnel shape, from wide to narrow, toward more specific questions, such as, "Tell me your reactions to how we studied *Romeo and Juliet.*"

Follow a preplanned format in every interview, especially when you seek to accumulate and compare answers of several individuals. Allow time too for side-tracking to learn about things you did not include in your interview plan. Make ample use of probes to elicit rich data: "Tell me more about that." "Give me an example of what you have in mind." "What, in particular, are you thinking about?" "How did you feel when that happened?"

Focus Group Formal Interviews

Bring to the interview sheets of heavy paper to make into name tents. Ask students to put their name on one side of a folded tent and to place their name tent in front of them for everyone to see. Use a round table, if possible. Make the interview appear formal, as though it could take place on television or National Public Radio. Ham it up.

Start with broad questions. Move from one student to another, calling each by name, expecting each to answer the same question in order. Gradually ask more specific questions. Strive to elicit responses from everyone on every question by calling on students by name. Turn your face and body to and fro; move from one student to another. Accept each answer without hesitation. Write answers down in front of the group on a poster, or ask two students to do that on a chalkboard. Use a recorder with the group's permission if that seems appropriate. Probe to get all students to speak. "Mary, how do you see that?" And "Paul, how do you see that?" "Judy, how about you?" and so on. Or ask, "Steve, do you have similar or different views about that? Tell me more!" and so on.

Be forewarned that focus group formal interviews take time. Remember too that they can be stimulating learning opportunities for students, especially the quiet ones. Use them as a natural and integral part of class. Look for ways to interview focus groups while other students are working at computers or at their desks doing solo assignments. You could interview groups of younger students sitting in a circle on a rug while other students are busy doing something with an aide.

If you sense that students are reluctant to speak up in front of you, ask a student to act as executive secretary and invite the group to hold a private discussion while you work with other students. Tell the appointed secretary to print a list of responses with no name attached so that every response is anonymous.

Interviews are useful to

- Establish rapport and empathy while collecting data
- Probe into students' subjective states about the class
- Obtain information from students who do not easily write about their thoughts and feelings
- Use students' remarks to stimulate contributions from other students

Figure 4.2 highlights the advantages and disadvantages of interviews.

Figure 4.2   Advantages vs. Disadvantages of Interviews

Advantages	Disadvantages
The data collector can probe for clarification and elaboration.	They are time consuming.
The data collector can build rapport and closeness with respondents.	The challenge of proper sampling arises when everyone can't be interviewed.
They can help in collecting data from respondents who cannot or will not write about their thoughts and feelings.	There is a lack of respondents' anonymity.
Respondents are anonymous when they pool answers outside earshot of the data collector.	The data collectors' physical characteristics and social position may lead to bias in respondents' answers.
Data can be gathered via audiotapes.	Respondents may fear that what they say will be used against them.

Observations

Observers attentively watch and record what they see and hear in a specific setting. They make either direct or mediated observations. To make direct observations, observers are present to see, hear, and record what takes place. With mediated observations, observers watch videotapes or listen to audiotapes of recorded events.

Direct and mediated observations vary in their structure or lack of structure. In structured observations, observers count how often particular behaviors occur; they focus their observations on a limited set of categories. In unstructured observations, observers do not use preplanned categories but remain open to the process flow and later search for themes in their observation record.

In your action research with students, ask colleagues or a few students, who temporarily sit on the side, to act as direct observers. Give them a list of categories if you want to structure their observations, or ask them to watch what happens, to take notes, and then to discuss and decide on the most important things they saw or heard. For student observers, that can be an unforgettable learning opportunity.

When using objective observers who sit off to the side, you will find that your research will be more effective if you focus their observations on 8 to 14 categories and you give them a time frame. For example, every five seconds the observers might check one of these categories: (1) you give information, (2) you state your feelings, (3) you ask a question, (4) you answer a question, (5) a student gives information, (6) a student speaks about feelings, (7) a student asks a question, (8) a student answers a question, (9) off-task behaviors, and (10) none of the above.

You can see, in that example, why it is not feasible for you to be a direct observer using a structured category system when you do your own action research. Should you design class times, however, when students manage themselves, such as cooperative projects in which every student is engaged in a small group discussion, then you could act as a direct observer with a structured list of categories. Still, the most efficient way to do structured observations on your own class is to watch videotapes or listen to audiotapes of recorded classroom events.

You can successfully carry out unstructured, direct observations by being sensitive to what is happening in class, by jotting down notes soon after class is finished, and then later recording a fuller description in your journal. Such unstructured direct observations can contribute significantly to action research and be relatively painless in the time they take. In proactive action research, try to be sensitive to your students' reactions to the new practice; in responsive action research, try to be aware of your students' nonverbal behaviors as they respond to data collections early in the project.

Observant Participation

Traditional researchers often use the term *participant observation* to label what you do when you make observations in your own class. That term has been used to label "scientific observers" to a third-world culture or to a modern community. Social anthropologists also use it to study "primitive cultures," and sociologists use it to study "modern communities." I prefer the related label, *observant participation*, to refer to teachers who observe in their own classes or to administrators who observe in their own schools. You are not curious visitors; you are participating members.

Two broad questions confront the observant participant: (1) What should you observe? and (2) How should you record the observations?

To answer the first query, list your hopes and concerns, central to both action research models. Your hopes are your project goals, and your concerns are your project's obstacles to success. Focus your unstructured direct observations on movements toward or away from your hopes and on how you deal with or do not deal with your concerns.

Several answers can be given to the second question. First, make available, for your easy access, notepads, index cards, or Post-it notes on which you have written symbols representing your hopes and concerns. You might have them color coded, numbered, or lettered for every hope and concern. Use them to jot down your observations while the class is proceeding or at interstitial moments between changes within or between classes. Second, keep a journal that you organize according to your hopes and concerns. Reflect and write in it once or twice a week for 30 minutes each time. Third, ask a critical friend (see Chapter 7), with whom you communicate often, to discuss observations with you about how the action research is proceeding.

Structured Observations

Structured observations, when carried out well, are more objective than unstructured observations; however, they typically are narrow and focused. Some consider them more valid, yet narrower, because precise questions are posed by well-defined categories. You ask very specific questions associated with your hopes, for example, "Did girls or boys speak more?" "Did black students ask as many questions as white students?" "Did students' time on task increase?" "Did I spend more or less time dealing with misbehaviors?" "Did cooperative learning groups perform better?" or "Was I more or less supportive of students during writer's workshop?"

A structured observation system, useful for many years in traditional research, is Amidon's verbal interaction system (see Schmuck and Schmuck, 2001, for details). His system has 12 categories, an efficient number for valid counting, which measure teacher-initiated talk (four categories), teacher-responses (two categories), student-responses (two categories), student-initiated talk (two categories), and other (two categories). Use Amidon's categories to check on how you and your students communicate during whole-class instruction. His instrument is one of hundreds of systematic observation formats that you can apply to action research.

The enhanced precision in structured observation arises because it allows you to quantify your data. To quantify data, which is especially helpful when you wish to validate the worth of a new practice, use a limited set of observation categories, specify the units of interaction you will record, and set time intervals for which entries will be made into the category system. To be practical, use structured observations three ways in your action research:

1. Train students in a class or teachers at faculty meetings to observe specific categories of interactions during particular periods of time. Make observing a learning experience.

2. Have older students, like middle schoolers or high schoolers, who are already tutors, helpers, or teaching assistants, make structured observations of new practices you are trying with younger students.

3. Enlist colleagues' help to make structured observations or have an administrator watch for specific categories of interaction during a regular supervision visit.

Figure 4.3   Advantages vs. Disadvantages of Observations

Advantages	Disadvantages
The data collector can gather data about behaviors, rather than just perceptions and feelings.	The data collector's presence can alter the respondents' behavior.
The data collector can see things that some respondents will not be able to report.	The data collectors might have to wait a long time before seeing what they seek to observe.
Data can be gathered via video.	Different data collectors might see different things while observing the same events.

Observations can be useful to

- Check for nonverbal expressions of students' feelings
- See which students play together, walk together between classes, and sit together at lunch, assemblies, or extracurricular events
- Grasp how students communicate with one another during group discussions or cooperative group projects
- Check how much time students spend on particular tasks
- Understand how you communicate with students with different characteristics at different times and contexts

Figure 4.3 highlights the advantages and disadvantages of observations.

Documents

Documents relevant to action research are school records, newspaper clippings, and private journals or diaries. School districts usually have public records about students, staffs, parents, and their boards.

For students, districts keep records of their scores on standardized assessments, such as state or regional tests in math and language arts; records of their rates of being absent, tardy, disciplined, retained, and suspended; records on their awards and achievements; and data that are aggregated by grade about students' performances on achievement tests and rates of leaving school and graduating with diplomas.

About school staffs, many districts keep minutes of faculty meetings and records of professional development events for the faculty. Also, many districts keep records of staff and role changes in the schools and district office from year to year, including rates of staff turnover.

About parents, many districts keep records of attendance rates at PTA meetings, parent-teacher conferences, and school open houses.

About boards, most districts keep records of board meeting agendas and of board decisions about school district policies. Some also keep data on citizens' rates of attendance and participation at district board meetings.

Newspaper clippings and personal journals or diaries can also contribute documentary data to your action research. Often community newspapers report on

Figure 4.4   Advantages vs. Disadvantages of Documents

Advantages	Disadvantages
Data are unaffected by the data collector's presence.	Records might be incomplete or amassed in biased ways.
Historical events can be studied objectively.	It is difficult to check on the validity of the information.

school events, such as board meetings, students' public performances, faculty members' biographical information, and students' achievements in extracurricular activities. Journals or diaries kept regularly by students, teachers, and administrators can also contribute valuable data to action research. You must, of course, guarantee journal authors that you will keep information confidential and that you will solicit written informed consent from the authors before using their data.

With documents, you use content analysis or coding to uncover recurring themes and multiple meanings. Content analysis is an objective, systematic, and quantitative description of written products. You can, for example, use content analysis to uncover themes and messages that are being presented to students via curriculum materials, textbooks, reading assignments, and your lesson plans. You also can apply it to your lectures and to your administrators' speeches and statements at formal meetings.

Figure 4.4 highlights the advantages and disadvantages of documents.

SPECIAL ISSUES OF ACTION RESEARCH

Three special issues arise when you do action research. First are the psychometric challenges of validity, reliability, and precision. Second are the psychological obstacles of lack of confidence, fear of failure, and overly high aspirations. Third are the process pitfalls that will inevitably arise while you implement the action research steps.

Psychometric Challenges

The excellence of your action research depends on the effectiveness of your new practice and on the accuracy of your data. To enhance data accuracy, build in your own mix of valid research procedures to produce credible and trustworthy data that are distortion free.

Enhance the validity of your research methods by (1) using at least two of the four primary methods (i.e., questionnaires, interviews, observations, and documents) to measure each variable under study, (2) specifying precisely your key variables by dissecting your hopes and concerns for the new practice, (3) adapting for your project validated methods from traditional research to measure your variables, (4) representing accurately the multiple perspectives of the participants in your project (i.e., students, parents, teachers, noncertificated staff, administrators, and community members), and (5) offering easy-to-understand visual or auditory data, with photographs, videos, recordings, films, charts, graphs, and figures.

A frequently cited threat to validity is the unreliability of research procedures. Unreliability occurs when the same methods, administered by several people or in different settings, produce different data. Examples relevant to your action research are (1) different responses on a questionnaire when it is completed in the classroom and at home, (2) different responses when two interviewers use the same interview procedure, (3) different data from observations when two observers watch the same event, and (4) different data from two coders who analyze the same document.

Tips for overcoming reliability threats and for enhancing validity are as follows:

- Keep questionnaires simple and short, asking participants to complete them in 30 minutes or less.
- Have participants in the same subgroups (i.e., students, parents, teachers, etc.) fill out the same questionnaire at the same time in the same setting.
- Have interviewers practice before carrying out formal interviews by role-playing with one another and then by doing at least one pilot-test interview together.
- Have observers record the same pilot-test events two times, and after each trial to discuss and resolve their discrepancies.
- Ask coders to analyze the content of two short documents, and after each analysis to discuss their discrepancies to resolve them.

Do the best you can to develop credible and trustworthy data. Do not worry excessively, however, about validity and reliability in your action research. Remember that your interest is in understanding what is actually happening with the processes and outcomes of your new practice. That is a focused and personal interest. Seek to achieve your hopes and to deal effectively with your concerns within the context of your own classroom, school, and district.

In action research, do not try to generalize beyond your own situation or your own new practices. Your interest is in internal validity, not external validity. Seek to create your own, local best practices by using sound scientific methods as guides to positive local action. Your challenge is to create your own unique package of the four research methods to enhance change in your own situation.

Psychological Obstacles

More serious challenges to doing action research well lie less in psychometrics and more in the mind-set you bring to it. If you are like me, you do not often admit to yourself that, as a certified professional, how you teach can be significantly improved. We typically do not dwell on our pedagogical shortcomings. I believe that a lack of openness to change is itself a serious weakness. Get in touch with yourself by brainstorming a list of shortcomings in your classes. You do not reach all the goals you hope for with all of your students all of the time. Write a solitary dialogue between your confident self and your doubting or critical self.

You might become aware of a few of your shortcomings but still resist initiating action research because you lack confidence in your capability to do research well. After all, you say to yourself, I chose to become a teacher, not a researcher. So remember that action research is a perspective and an activity that you integrate into your teaching plans. Like Robert Hess's (1996) research on his writer's workshop, your data collection and analysis should be an integral part of your lesson plan. The research is not an add-on; it is an *enriched lesson plan*.

Perhaps you see how data collections and analyses can become integral to your regular teaching, but you may be too grandiose in your ambition for the research. You may want to do too much and to achieve too many hopes with a single project. Think small, be focused, especially in your first action research effort. Like Hess, focus on a single practice in a single class. Give yourself permission to change your professional practice one small step by one small step.

Process Pitfalls

To get started right with action research in your own mind does not guarantee success. You will confront pitfalls or setbacks as you implement the steps, because even the most narrowly focused design engages diverse participants and multiple audiences.

Since you are doing new and different activities with your students, they will react variously. Some may become upset with the new actions if they do not understand why you are doing things differently from what they expected. Tell them what you hope to accomplish, why you need their help, how important this new project is to you, and how everyone will benefit from the data collections. Bring your key administrators and a few key colleagues on board early. Tell them how excited you are about the potential benefits of action research. Tell the students' parents about the project and how it will benefit their daughters and sons. Believe in the project's potentialities; involve students every step of the way.

A serious potential pitfall is that the action research process will take time away from the required curriculum and testing program. Think seriously about time before you start the action research. Think up hopes that merge with school goals and district values. Design new practices and data collections that fit into your required curriculum and regular instructional strategies. Plan for meaningful ways in which students' work on data collections and analyses become integral to the curriculum.

Students, colleagues, administrators, and parents will trust you about the usefulness of the action research for student learning and school improvement unless they think you are doing the project primarily to feather your own nest. Perceptions like that often arise when you use the research to satisfy a requirement for a degree. If you plan to do that, clearly differentiate between action research activities integral to your instruction and activities you are required to do to complete the college requirement. Keep the former activities in the school; do the latter activities outside school in the evenings or on weekends and during vacations.

THE ETHICS OF ACTION RESEARCH

Ethics are principles of moral values and right conduct. Ethics in action research focus on your moral relationships to the participants (e.g., students, educators, and parents). Since your action research is local and focused on whole persons who are known to one another, the imperative for you to be ethical is pressing. Your ethical bottom line is that no student, or any other participant, is harmed by the action research, and since continuous improvement is your overarching goal, your students ought to benefit. That sets the ethical bar of action research higher than the ethical bar for traditional research. Will your students benefit by taking part in the project?

Adhere to ten specific ethical principles as you carry out your action research. You should

1. Obtain data only about variables related to the specific project. To be ethical, focus your data collection on your project's context (e.g., descriptions of the community, the district, the school, your class, etc.), your specific target groups (e.g., numbers, age ranges, grade levels, sex, race, etc.), your hopes (i.e., goals and outcomes), and your concerns (i.e., perceived pitfalls and obstacles).

2. Discuss the research plan with administrators, colleagues, and appropriate boards so that they provide legitimacy.

3. Obtain the informed consent of participants and their agreement to take part by summarizing project purposes, procedures, and hoped for outcomes.

4. Relate to participants with care and respect by connecting with them as whole persons rather than as research subjects. That is the heart and soul of action research.

5. Keep data confidential on individual participants.

6. Do not disclose data publicly without the consent of the participants.

7. Inform parents and other community members in order to develop public legitimacy for the project.

8. Strive to integrate the action research into your everyday, primary tasks so that it supports them rather than interferes with your regular professional work. That is the credo of the mature educator.

9. Report research findings to students and to relevant administrators, colleagues, boards, parents, and community members.

10. Seek ways to continue the action research with additional cycles of positive action and meaningful research.

Reflections

Reflect on Chapter 4 by answering the following questions:

1. When you wish to detect how one of your practices is working, what research methods would you prefer to use?

2. When you want to judge the *merit* or the *worth* of one of your practices, what research methods would you prefer to use?

3. What do you think you should do to enhance the validity of your research methods?

4. What might you do to avoid the obstacles and the pitfalls of action research projects?

5. What do you consider are the most important ethical principles to keep in mind as you do action research?

5

Proactive Action Research

If you have built castles in the air, your work need not be lost; there is where they should be. Now put foundations under them.

—Henry David Thoreau ([1854] 1937)

I tried the writer's workshop with tenth graders to give them more choice and freedom in what and how they write and to help them become more effective writers.

—Robert Hess (1996)

Hess's action research was proactive because his new practice, writer's workshop for tenth graders (see Chapter 2), grew out of his own reflections from professional reading and classroom experiences. He believed that his traditional method of direct instruction in writing was not helping students develop favorable attitudes toward writing, nor was it building their self-confidence as writers. Instead, he thought that his students were turned off, more and more, to writing and that he would try another teaching method.

Marilyn Lund, a new teacher, and James Johnson, a mature teacher, both realized that they also needed to try new teaching methods. Marilyn carried out proactive action research by herself in her sixth-grade class. Like Robert Hess, Marilyn focused primarily on her own professional development as an effective teacher. James engaged the students of his eighth-grade social studies class as partners in carrying out cooperative, proactive action research. James encouraged and helped his students create new ways to improve their classroom climate.

MARILYN LUND*

Marilyn Lund graduated from college with a BA in sociology and two varsity letters in tennis at age 25. After two years coaching adults in an athletic club, she decided to earn a master's degree in elementary education and a teacher's license. She was interested in the upper elementary grades, believing she was not effective with very young children. Now, as she turns 31, she has completed a first year of teaching sixth grade at River Grove Elementary School.

Although her first year as a teacher was not a total failure (she will return to River Grove for a second year of probationary teaching), Marilyn wonders if perhaps she should have become a high school teacher. She feels frustrated with her principal because he did not help her better understand 11-year-olds. She is also angry with herself for not doing a better job of starting the class last September. She remembers her wish to go fast and to put emphasis on homework and on academic excellence. Something went wrong from the start.

Last May, the principal rated Marilyn as "adequate" on most scales during her evaluation but did rate her as "above average" in social studies and physical education. Those two subjects were her favorite to teach. The worst of it was that the principal rated her as "needs to improve" in classroom management, student rapport, and student discipline. She vividly recalls—even today, three months after the event—how strongly the principal pleaded with her to build more positive discipline into her teaching. "Marilyn," he said, "try to cut down on the negative with your students. Accentuate the positive. Play to their strengths." Now, after a summer of playing tennis, attending a five-day workshop on cooperative learning, and reading a book on classroom group processes, Marilyn will start teaching 28 sixth graders at River Grove in a few weeks.

Marilyn Reflects on Her Practice

As Marilyn reflects, let us listen in on her solitary dialogue about her practice. Marilyn's past self thinks: "I wasn't ready to be positive with and supportive of students last year. I was too concerned with my own security and self-esteem. I felt insecure, even scared, about working every day with 11-year-olds. I didn't want to lose control of them, nor did I want to look incompetent to my colleagues or to the principal. I felt relieved when the principal didn't observe my class for the first ten weeks."

Marilyn's future self thinks: "I want very much to conduct my class differently this year. First, I want to heed my principal's advice to be more positive with the students. Also, I must worry less about myself and think more about how the students react to me. I plan to be much more observant of students' feelings this year. I want to accentuate the positive and to look for students' strengths."

Marilyn's past self thinks: "That's easy to think now, but when students don't follow my directions, I'll become cross and make hurtful remarks to them just like last year. At times last year I flew off the handle and actualized my worst fears by really losing control. Talk about the self-fulfilling prophecy. Will this year be any different?"

---

*All names of educators, schools, and communities have been changed.

Marilyn's future self thinks: "Yes, I'll change because I truly want to become a more effective sixth-grade teacher. After all, I've demonstrated my effectiveness many times teaching tennis to insecure adults. I also have demonstrated my effectiveness teaching sixth graders social studies and physical education. I can become a more caring teacher, because students' ideas and feelings are important to me. I know that I can become more receptive to students' ideas. I will listen more carefully than last year, strive to paraphrase students' ideas, and respect and show empathy for their feelings. I will use ideas I learned in the cooperative learning workshop this summer."

Marilyn's past self thinks: "A year ago, I didn't reflect and plan like I am now. Last September, I hardly thought about the 28 students and what they might be like as individuals. Last year, I primarily thought about the sixth-grade curriculum, student achievement, and students following my directions. I wonder if I'll be able to change those thought patterns."

Marilyn's future self thinks: "Yes, this year I'll think much more about establishing trusting relationships with students. I will not seek domination or control. This year, instead of power over my students I will strive to establish power with the students. Above all, I'll try to act warmer with students than I did last year. I shall try, also, to maintain a sense of humor and to laugh at my own mistakes. I want to be more open about my feelings and encourage students to share their feelings openly with me."

Marilyn's past self thinks: "That all sounds good, but like last year, I still think mostly about myself. Last year, I didn't have strategies to teach students respect for one another. I'm naive to think that changes in me alone will improve relationships in this year's class. Part of my problem last year was unfriendly relationships in the peer group. Lots of students felt rejected, neglected, or isolated from the most popular students. The students' negative feelings didn't only come from my actions; they were also communicated from student to student. How will I take peer group influences into account this year?"

Marilyn's Knowledge (and Methods) Search

Marilyn's future self thinks: "This year, during the first few weeks of school, I plan to carry out a series of positive, get-acquainted, team-building activities that I learned this summer. I learned about ways to establish trust and cohesiveness with sixth graders. I experienced a number of useful exercises and procedures in my workshop on cooperative learning and found some wonderful action ideas for improving classroom climate in the text on classroom group processes (Schmuck and Schmuck 2001). I'll use information I got in the workshop and through my reading to improve peer group relationships as well as my rapport with the students.

"I'll relax more than last year. I will not push the academic curriculum so hard during the first few weeks of class. Also, I'll appoint a committee of four to six students to help me monitor how the students feel about my teaching and about the peer group climate. I'll call that committee our Sixth-Grade Steering Committee, like the teacher did who was described in the text I studied. I'll tell the class a little about how quality circles function in business and how the steering committee will act like a quality circle. Membership on the steering committee will change every three weeks to give everyone a chance to participate during the first semester. I'll also facilitate whole-class discussions to make group agreements on how we will work together in our class. I intend for all students to set the class rules."

Marilyn's past self thinks: "Those plans sound fine, but how will I know if they work? Last year, I didn't realize how bad the students' feelings were until the principal observed the class in November. After he gave me feedback, I became defensive, wondering why he took so long to visit my class. I didn't want to believe him. Also, by that time it was hard to modify the peer group patterns that had formed."

Marilyn's future self thinks: "This year I'll be more conscious of students' reactions than I was last year. Along with my daily observations of classroom interaction, which I'll write about in a journal, I'll also regularly interview members of the steering committee about how the class is going, as I was taught to do in my summer workshop. Furthermore, I found simple questionnaires in the text that I'll use with the students to receive feedback from everyone about how 'I' and 'we' are doing. Now I believe that I'm ready to tackle the new academic year. I already feel good about this year, my second year of teaching."

Marilyn begins the year with new vigor.

Marilyn's Hopes and Concerns

Marilyn's hopes are that the students will

- Get to know and appreciate one another
- Feel respect toward one another
- Value the different strengths and talents of one another
- Cooperate in sharing constructive leadership with her
- Solve interpersonal problems and resolve conflicts with one another
- Support one another in learning their academic subjects together

In contrast, Marilyn's concerns are that a few students will

- Act impolitely, perhaps aggressively, toward their peers
- Feel rejected, ignored, or isolated from their peers
- Refuse to follow group agreements, even when all students make the agreements
- Show a lack of focus on academic learning for sustained blocks of time

With this mix of hopes and concerns, Marilyn carries out the new classroom practices.

Marilyn's New Practices

Marilyn decides on three new get-acquainted practices for the first weeks of class:

1. A human resource hunt in which she gives each student a list of experiences, attributes, and hobbies. The students hunt for classmates who have those "resources."

2. Student biographies in which pairs of students interview each other about important life experiences. Each student writes a two-page biography of his or her partner. Over the next nine days of class, Marilyn asks the students to read the biographies to the class.

3. A Tinkertoy construction in which groups of five students construct a symbolic representation of what they hope their classroom climate will be like in a few weeks.

During the second week, Marilyn establishes the first steering committee. She tells the committee that her goal is for the students to help her in managing the class so they can all share in a supportive and healthy climate. She picks three girls and three boys with very different levels of academic ability for the first committee. She announces that all students will eventually serve as steering committee members. Marilyn works with the initial steering committee every day during lunch for one week, training its members to understand and use the task and social-emotional group roles. After the week of training, the steering committee meets with Marilyn twice a week to discuss problems, goals, and possible rules for classroom behavior and work.

After three weeks, Marilyn and the steering committee present their ideas about rules and procedures to the class; they are discussed and voted on by everyone. Next, six new members are appointed to be the second steering committee. By the end of the first semester, the class—with the help of its steering committees—has created a list of classroom rules and procedures. As the year progresses, the steering committees help Marilyn solve discipline problems and keep the class focused on academic learning. The class decides to use the term *Group Agreements*, instead of *Rules*. Read Schmuck and Schmuck (2001) for details.

Marilyn Collects Data

Marilyn uses three methods to detect how the new practices affect the students.

First, she carefully observes students' reactions to the get-acquainted activities to make certain that every student's strengths and talents are publicly stated. She also watches herself and increases positive statements as she strives to be supportive. Every other day, Marilyn writes in a journal about her observations of the students and herself. The reflective writing gives Marilyn opportunities to continue solitary dialogues about her professional values and practices throughout the year.

Second, Marilyn interviews members of the steering committee, one-on-one and as a group. She asks, "How do you think our class is going? Do you see any problems that we should try to solve? In what ways do you think our class could be improved? Are there changes you would like me to make? What ideas do you have to help all students learn more and better? What can we do as a class to help each of you learn math better, social studies better, language arts better, and so on?"

Third, Marilyn uses a questionnaire in mid-October to assess how "I" and "we" are doing. To obtain data about herself as a teacher, she uses a questionnaire, titled Our Teacher, in which she asks students to check one of the following scale points: much more, a little more, the same, a little less, or much less. The students rate Marilyn on the following behaviors: helps with work, yells at us, smiles and laughs, makes us behave, trusts us on our own, makes sure our work is done, asks us to decide, and makes us work hard. Figure 5.1 shows the entire Our Teacher questionnaire.

To collect data about the class as a group, Marilyn uses a questionnaire titled Clues About Classroom Life in which she encourages students to act like detectives and write answers to the following open-ended questions: "What are some clues to a good day in this class? What things happen that are signs of a good day? What are

Figure 5.1   Our Teacher

Pretend that I (your teacher) could change the ways I relate to you in school. For each number, check the box that best tells how you would like me to act in this class.

	Much more	A little more	The same	A little less	Much less
1. Helps with work					
2. Yells at us					
3. Smiles and laughs					
4. Makes us behave					
5. Trusts us on our own					
6. Makes sure our work is done					
7. Asks us to decide					
8. Makes us work hard					

Source: Adapted from *Group Processes in the Classroom*, 8th edition (Schmuck and Schmuck 2001:103). Reprinted with permission from McGraw-Hill Companies, Inc.

some clues to a bad day in this class? What things happen that are clues that this class is not going the way it should or the way that you would like it to? What are some things that should happen a lot more than they do to make this class a better place for learning?" Figure 5.2 shows the entire Clues About Classroom Life questionnaire.

Marilyn Checks on What the Data Mean

Marilyn uses four methods to check what the data mean.

First, she writes her reflections in a journal and rereads them from time to time. She reflects on the past, present, and future. Now and then, she reflects on whether she is reaching her hopes and on how she is dealing with her concerns.

Second, Marilyn holds discussions once a week with the steering committee, where she presents some of the data she collects. She gives her own analysis and interpretation, then checks to see if students agree or disagree with her findings. She encourages students to join her in the detection and judgment phases of the action research.

Third, Marilyn informally meets once every two weeks with a close friend who teaches fifth graders at another school in the same district. While they eat dinner, they talk about what they do in their classes and the reactions they get from their students. Afterward, Marilyn writes in her journal ideas and reactions she has received from her friend.

Fourth, Marilyn formally meets with the principal once a month to talk about how her class is going. She tells the principal about her new practices, invites him to observe, and describes the data she has collected. Marilyn and the principal talk about how to keep students focused on academic learning while maintaining a positive classroom climate. The principal is pleased with Marilyn's creativity and professional maturity.

Figure 5.2   Clues About Classroom Life

So that we may get some ideas about how to make life more interesting and important for everybody in this class, each of us needs to contribute ideas about what should be improved. What things happen that shouldn't happen? What ought to happen that does not? Imagine you are a detective looking for clues to a "good day" and a "bad day" in this class. Jot down what you might look for or might see to answer these questions.

What are some clues to a good day in this class? What things happen that are signs of a good day?

1. _____
2. _____
3. _____
4. _____

What are some clues to a bad day in this class? What things happen that are clues that this class is not going the way it should or the way that you would like it to?

5. _____
6. _____
7. _____
8. _____

What are some things that should happen a lot more than they do to make this class a better place for learning?

9. _____
10. _____
11. _____
12. _____

Marilyn Reflects on Alternative Ways to Behave

Marilyn uses the data feedback sessions with her students and discussions with her friend and the principal to dream about alternative ways to teach. While she is pleased with the success of her new practices, Marilyn sees how they could be improved next time. For instance, although a few biographies were outstanding, many were too short, some were poorly written, and a few were inaccurate. Some students asked 14 or 15 questions, while other students asked only 2 or 3 questions. Marilyn realizes that she should have helped students generate a standard list of interview questions and that the whole class should have created a standard outline for the biographies. Similar problems did not arise with the human resource hunt or the Tinkertoy construction, because she prepared a standard list of 20 resources for the hunt and had each group of students work with the same number of Tinkertoys.

Upon reflection of the strengths and weaknesses of the steering committees, Marilyn decides she will start next year's steering committee during the first week and spread out work on the biographies over the first three weeks. Also, Marilyn ponders whether she should form all steering committees from the start so that all students know they will get a chance to work closely with Marilyn to govern the class. Furthermore, her preformed steering committees could serve as basic support groups for cooperative learning projects. Marilyn decides to discuss these ideas with her friend and the principal.

SCHOOL OF EDUCATION
CURRICULUM LABORATORY
UM-DEARBORN

Marilyn Fine-Tunes Her New Practice

Marilyn decides to ask students to prepare another biography after the winter holiday. She forms students into groups of four. Her task is for each small group to create a fictitious biography of a make-believe person who has six personal characteristics of each student member in the group. In other words, the fictitious character that each group creates will have a total of 24 characteristics—six actual qualities of each group member. Marilyn leads the whole class in discussions about the sorts of personal characteristics that might make up the biographies. She is pleased with the students' enthusiasm for the biography and looks forward to positive results.

Marilyn is fully involved in proactive action research and will continue the creative process throughout the year.

JAMES JOHNSON*

After graduating with a BA in history and a secondary-teacher certificate, James went to work at Arlington High School. He taught world and American history to 10th and 11th graders for ten years and served as an assistant coach for boys' football and as head coach of girls' track and field. Five years ago, James and the girls' track team took second place in the state track finals.

Changing demographics in the Arlington community meant that the number of 10th, 11th, and 12th graders was in decline, while the number of elementary youngsters was increasing. The new demographics in Arlington called for K–5 elementary schools, 6–8 middle schools, and a 9–12 high school. The Arlington School District changed from a three-year to a four-year senior high school, creating two new middle schools to replace its one large junior high school. James and seven colleagues from the former high school were transferred to the middle schools. Although James did not want to leave the high school, he also did not wish to move from Arlington. So he reluctantly agreed to teach eighth-grade social studies at Jacobs Middle School. The results of his first year of middle school teaching were terrible. Now he's a middle school teacher, no longer a coach, and frustrated with his job.

James Searches for Knowledge

James decides to return to school in the summer to pursue a master's degree in school administration. He never thought about administration before, but in the face of his most frustrating year ever as a teacher, he decides administration might be a good idea for him. He thinks that he could use the added salary and that his coaching experience has prepared him for management and leadership. He decides to get his feet wet before diving into graduate school and takes only two courses—Educational Leadership and Alternative Models of Teaching.

James finds that the two courses complement each other. Both give a good deal of attention to group work. In the Educational Leadership course, he is introduced to the skills of organization development, participatory management, and democratic leadership. In the Alternative Models of Teaching course, James learns about cooperative learning and cross-age tutoring. He writes a term paper about using

---

*All names of educators, schools, and communities have been changed.

cooperative learning in social studies, and he reads a few research reports on the benefits of older students tutoring younger students. He decides to try out some of these strategies in his own eighth-grade social studies classes in the fall. He has found what he needs most—not new energy for school administration but new ideas to reinvigorate his teaching. He remembers why he loved coaching so much—the teamwork and the challenge of supporting one another in achieving excellence.

James's Reflections on His Practice

James's past self thinks: "In the past, to teach and to coach represented very different spheres of activity. When I taught, I lectured, asked specific questions about the text, drilled students for names and dates, assigned reading and workbook pages for homework, gave frequent tests, and assigned grades without giving students much helpful feedback. When I coached, I held discussions with the athletes, got to know them as individuals, sought to find out how they felt, encouraged them to do well, challenged them to improve, assigned groups of athletes to study their football plays or track relays together, and sought ways to give constructive feedback, even in the face of defeat."

James's future self thinks: "In the future—in fact in just a month or so—I want to teach middle school students like the coach I was, rather than the high school teacher I was. I want to use cooperative learning techniques instead of lecture and drill, and I want to increase the students' engagement with learning. I want to encourage them to become teachers of one another and of younger students. Teaching is a good way to learn. I will use Aronson's (1978) jigsaw puzzle method and the Sharan and Sharan (1992) group investigation method. (Each of these methods is explained in Figure 5.3.) I will also find an elementary teacher who wants to collaborate with me on a cross-age tutoring project." (For original literature about cross-age tutoring, read Lippitt and Lohman, 1965, and Lippitt, Eisman, and Lippitt, 1969.)

James conducts proactive action research, though not consciously, as did Marilyn. James's innovation also differs from Marilyn's in his decision to engage students as partners at every stage. James performs cooperative, proactive action research.

James's Hopes and Concerns

James's hopes are that

- The students will become turned on to social studies.
- He will feel renewed and reinvigorated in his teaching.
- The students will master the eighth-grade social studies curriculum.
- Students will learn to apply social science to topics of importance to them.
- The students will value helping one another learn.

James's concerns are that

- Quite a few students will not carry their load in cooperative learning.
- He might not have courage to stay the course if some students do not behave.
- Some students will not strive to apply social science to important topics.
- A few students might not relate well to younger students.

Figure 5.3 James's First Two New Practices

Aronson's Jigsaw Puzzle

Aronson (1978) created the jigsaw cooperative learning procedure to foster both interpersonal acceptance and student learning. Students teach one another portions of some curriculum content. They work in two sorts of small groups (e.g., learning teams and expert groups). Each learning team divides the curriculum content into equal portions so each member can teach a portion to the other members. Before students in learning teams teach one another, those students in the class with the same portions of content to teach meet together in expert groups to review the content and to discuss how they will each teach it to their respective learning teams.

Sharan and Sharan's Group Investigation

Sharan and Sharan (1992) created the group investigation method, which includes six steps:

1. A topic is specified and students are grouped into teams of six to do research on the topic.

2. The topic is divided into subtopics, and each member selects a subtopic for individual study.

3. Individuals report back to their team on what they have learned. The team, in turn, integrates all contributions into a single outline and report.

4. The team reports to the whole class.

5. Team reports are evaluated by peers, and modifications are made.

6. Teams turn their project reports in to the teacher for feedback and evaluation.

Even with those concerns in mind, James remains enthusiastic about the new practices he has chosen to initiate.

James Tries a New Practice

On the first class day, James tells the eighth graders about his reflections during the summer at the university. He describes how differently he acted as a teacher compared to how he acted as a coach. He tells the students he wants to act more like a facilitator and catalyst of their learning, rather than like a director and controller. He goes on to describe the three new practices he will use in this class:

1. Aronson's (1978) jigsaw puzzle method, a cooperative learning procedure to help everyone learn about the text and the workbook assignments

2. Sharan and Sharan's (1992) group investigation method, another form of cooperative learning to help everyone apply social studies information to topics important to them

3. Cross-age tutoring to help everyone learn how to help someone else to learn, which helps students learn about social responsibility and democratic citizenship

Every Friday, James and the class debrief how the "Johnson experiment" is proceeding. He solicits feedback from the students about how helpful or unhelpful the three new practices are for their learning. He makes changes in classroom procedures according to the wishes of the majority, so long as what the majority wants is legal, moral, ethical, and acceptable to district policy. "We shall study together," James tells the students, "ways to improve the climate of our class, so that every student has an opportunity to learn about social studies. We will learn about social studies through a study of our own social interaction."

James Creates Methods to Collect Data

Since James is engaging students as partners in change, this third step is at the heart of his project. Every Friday, for 50 minutes, he and the students study the three new practices together. James's primary research method is the focus group interview, during which he raises questions about the new practices. For example, while the class uses Aronson's jigsaw puzzle method to learn contents of the text, James asks, "What do you see in Aronson's jigsaw puzzle method that helps you learn the contents of the text? What is it about this method that doesn't help you learn the contents of the text? What are changes we might make in this method to enhance your learning of the contents of the text? Please brainstorm out loud about any other thoughts or feelings you have about this method." Instead of acting as sole interviewer, James often divides the students into pairs or trios so students can interview one another about the jigsaw puzzle method.

Prior to his initiation of Sharan and Sharan's group investigation method, James asks students to identify social issues and societal problems that are important to them. The content could be about the social effects of viewing television; whether aggression and hostility on the television or in the movies increases the viewer's aggressiveness; how relations are portrayed between races, ethnic groups, or sexes; how computers affect our lives; how aspects of the environment affect people's feelings; and so on. Once the class generates a list of topics, James asks the students to choose two topics that interest them. Next, he creates small groups of students with similar interests. At this time, Sharan and Sharan's group investigation method formally begins.

During the four weeks of the group investigation method, James uses debriefing time to ask students how the investigations are unfolding and how the project groups might be improved.

Before implementing cross-age tutoring, James and the students discuss how to be an effective tutor. Also, because the eighth graders are tutoring Sara Everton's second graders, James initiates discussions about seven-year-olds and what they are like. After the tutoring is under way, class discussions focus on the challenges of effective tutoring and, in particular, on how to tutor second graders who misbehave or seem out of control.

In contrast to Marilyn, who uses multiple methods to collect data, James collects most of his data with group interviews. James and his students also use unstructured direct observations, since all of them are observant participants. Although it might appear that Marilyn's mix of methods has more ingredients, the power of "consensual community" is actualized during James's debriefings. By pooling the observations of all participants, James obtains valid data, particularly as he engages every student in the discussions and does not make hasty judgments based on the ideas and perceptions of a few high-talking students. James increases the validity of his data by encouraging everyone to speak openly and honestly. He facilitates full participation by calling on every student for input.

James Checks on What the Data Mean

James uses three methods to check the meaning of the data he and the students generate.

First, he reflects on how the data match the concepts of group development, which he learned in his two summer graduate courses. He checks, in particular, whether students are appreciating one another's learning styles, sharing leadership functions, supporting one another to learn about social studies, and making constructive contributions to improve the new practices.

Second, James checks his data interpretations with the students' perceptions of the data. He presents the students' summaries of data he has analyzed and asks them about the accuracy or inaccuracy of his conclusions. He tries to focus these discussions on the here and now and probes students for their interpretations of what is currently happening in the class. He follows up with questions about how to improve the three new practices.

Third, James meets once a month with Sara Everton. James brings data about cross-age tutoring from his student debriefings, and Sara brings her observations of how the tutoring is affecting her second graders. Together, James and Sara think about how to improve the tutoring program.

James Reflects on Alternative Ways to Behave

From his discussions with the students and with Sara Everton, James generates ideas about how to improve the three practices.

He decides that smaller expert groups work better when using Aronson's jigsaw puzzle method. He decides to try expert groups of two or three instead of five. He also decides to ask all student-experts to prepare written summaries of their part of the text prior to the expert-group discussion. The first change increases airtime for each student in the expert groups. The second change increases students' accountability for studying the text before the expert-group meetings.

For Sharan and Sharan's group investigation method, James decides to reduce the size of the project groups from six to four to increase airtime and involvement of each group member.

For cross-age tutoring, James believes the eighth graders should receive more tutor training before their work with the second graders begins. He thinks the new training should include role playing and discussion of typical tutoring problems.

James Fine-Tunes His New Practice

At the start of the second semester, James's class moves to the computer lab, and a group of eighth graders that had been in computer lab in the fall moves into social studies with James. James decides to revise the three practices right away with this new class.

Along with the modifications he thought about in Step 5, James decides to try another new idea in cross-age tutoring. At a student debriefing, after his class completed two tutoring sessions with the second graders, James introduces a procedure he calls helping trios. He divides the class into groups of three and tells students that each trio has three roles: tutor, helper, and observer. The tutor asks for help in becoming an effective tutor. The helper aids the tutor in figuring out how to become more effective. James instructs the helpers in a problem-solving method. The observer reflects out loud on how the helper was or wasn't helpful to the tutor. The roles within the trios rotate so that each member performs all three roles a few times.

James likes the helping trios because they focus on tutoring about tutoring and help students view tutoring from three points of view. James feels renewed and looks forward to the rest of the year.

THE SIX STEPS OF PROACTIVE ACTION RESEARCH

The steps you take in proactive action research are interdependent, circular, and continuous. Your reflections and your knowledge search will typically feed each other. With thoughtful questioning, you can get ready to internalize new knowledge, and getting introduced to new knowledge can focus your thoughts on hopes and concerns. Figure 5.4 illustrates the connection between the steps and phases of proactive action research.

In proactive action research, creative problem solving and innovative practice precede data collection; however, your desire to risk doing something new often stems from past, preconscious data collections. Those preconscious thoughts and feelings take the form of nagging frustrations, unfulfilled dreams, and unexpressed wishes. They are the psychological foundations on which your search for new and better practice stands and the bases of your proactive action research.

Figure 5.4   The Six Steps of Proactive Action Research

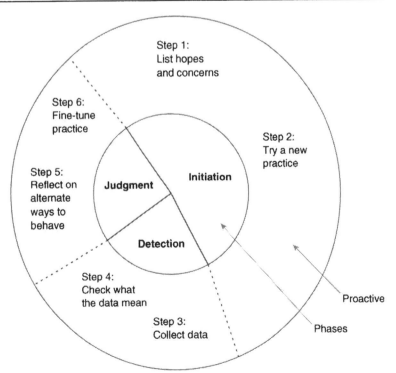

Step 1: List Hopes and Concerns

Each new practice should be instrumental in moving you and your class from the current situation to a preferred state in the future. Try to be explicit about your goals for the new practice and be realistic about obstacles.

When writing about hopes in a journal, use such verb constructions as *to achieve, to establish, to create, to facilitate, to foster, to lead to,* and *to produce.* When writing about concerns, use such verb constructions as *will accept, will be, will feel, will move away, will move toward, will reject,* and *will not want.* Although concerns might be supportive, neutral, or unsupportive in relation to hopes, give special attention to concerns about events that may prevent the hopes from being reached.

Step 2: Try a New Practice

Reflect on practices you want to initiate before trying them. Like Marilyn Lund, rehearse a solitary dialogue between your past and future selves. Or, like James Johnson, reflect in a solitary dialogue about how you want to act anew with your students. Think about your values, your unfulfilled dreams, and the sort of role model you want to be. Now, design the new practice.

If you're stuck and can't find a new practice, read two creative authors for ideas. Linda Campbell (2003) in *Mindful Learning* offers 101 best classroom practices grounded in traditional research, and Donna Walker Tileston (2005) presents an updated version of her classic, *Ten Best Teaching Practices.* Skim their books for good ideas of new practices.

The term *new practice* applies differently from one educator to another. A new practice to one teacher is an old practice to another, forsaken by another, and unrecognizable or out of sight to another.

Robert Hess's writer's workshop strategy was new to him, although hundreds of high school English teachers already use a form of it. Probably thousands of others don't know what it is, and perhaps a handful of others have tried and forsaken it.

Naturally, a host of classroom practices were new to Marilyn, who had taught for only a short time. Nevertheless, her idea to use the get-acquainted activities that she learned in a workshop is out of sight and out of mind to thousands of elementary teachers.

James's use of cooperative learning was new to him, although hundreds of middle school teachers have used cooperative learning methods for over a decade. It's likely that the majority of middle school teachers, however, don't know about Aronson's jigsaw puzzle method or Sharan and Sharan's group investigation method—practices that Johnson learned at summer school.

Step 3: Search for Methods and Collect Data

The research begins now with collecting formal data. You can use questionnaires, interviews, observations, or documents. Your hopes and concerns guide the content of the data collections. The data help assess whether progress is being made toward your desired goals and whether your anticipated pitfalls are being avoided.

Before you create the data collection instruments for your study, search for methods in others' action research. Search using terms like *action research methods, collaborative action research, school-based action research,* and *teacher research.* Go directly to search engines such as Google and Yahoo! Also, a number of chapters of recent texts could jump-start your thinking about instruments.

R. Murray Thomas (2003, chap. 5) offered a useful discussion on data collection processes and instruments and gave information about content analysis, observations, interviews, questionnaires, and academic tests. Richard Sagor (2005, chap. 7) gives information about data collection, as does Geoffrey Mills (2003, chap. 3). Look too at my books about classrooms and schools for examples of instruments for data collection. In Schmuck and Runkel (1994), read Chapters 4–8 for ways of gathering data about communication, meetings, problem solving, decision making, and conflict. In Schmuck and Schmuck (2001), review the 25 instruments to measure aspects of classroom interaction. Also read Walker (1985) for tips on useful methods for the teacher researcher.

Because your effort to try new practices is unique, however, create your own data collection instruments. James did that when he thought of the open-ended questions he used in the student debriefings. Ask about and observe your hopes and concerns. You are a better judge of the questions to use than a university-based researcher or an author of a traditional book on social science methods. Still, others' research instruments can be put to use. Marilyn adapted others' questionnaire ideas to create the questionnaires she called Our Teacher and Clues About Classroom Life. The point is to use data collection techniques that enhance your own professional maturity and the growth and development of your students.

Step 4: Check on What the Data Mean

Raw data are merely numbers and words. They become useful when integrated into reflections on the past, present, and future. They take on meaning when they help answer questions about the merit and worth of new practices. Although fresh personal insight can be gained by silently reflecting on the data, group discussions about the data also help. Remember G. H. Mead's idea about the integral association between thinking and social interaction? The data of action research become most useful when incorporated into conversations about teaching practices with important others.

Perhaps the most important audience for conversations about the data is the classroom group itself. As James demonstrated, partnering with students offers a good way to check what the data mean. In James's classes, students not only learned about social studies through cooperative group work, but they also learned about social studies by doing a scientific study of James's social experiment. They experienced social science by doing action research on their social studies curriculum.

Other appropriate partners to interact with about the meaning of the data include

- A teacher friend outside your school
- A trusted colleague within your school
- Parents of students
- A small team of colleagues
- A principal

Step 5: Reflect on Alternative Ways to Behave

Think of the meanings gleaned from the data in Step 4. What conclusions were drawn from conversations about the data? Are there some consistent themes that cut across those conversations? Now think of the day-to-day reflections on how the new practices unfolded. No information from others can substitute for your own reflection on the present about how the students are reacting. This is one reason why writing in a journal often and regularly can be helpful. The combination of others' understandings of the data and your own interpretations of what happened determine alternative ways to behave in the future.

Step 6: Fine-Tune the New Practice

You have now returned to the beginning. Either implement new practices with your current students or look for a fresh start with new student groups. Either way, one cycle of proactive action research has been completed, and you have combined action research with reflection and problem solving.

THE RANGE OF PROACTIVE MODELS

Marilyn Lund and James Johnson focused their proactive initiatives on the social-emotional lives of their students. Robert Hess also was interested in how his students felt about writing, but he put more emphasis on his students' writing performance. In those three projects, we have instances of proactive action research in elementary, middle, and senior high school.

Margo O'Neill (2004), while studying for a graduate degree in education, wrote library research papers about reading curriculum for primary students. That work convinced her that the Spalding (2003) method, a multisensory strategy for teaching six-, seven-, and eight-year-olds to write, spell, and read, could work well in her own school. Her academic knowledge became more personal when she saw her son blossom as a reader after he received one-on-one coaching by a Spalding tutor.

As her school's director, she worked closely with six primary teachers and their classes to implement action research on the Spalding method. The project lasted for an entire year; she demonstrated that while most students benefited with significant growth in spelling and reading, the second graders benefited the most. After several summertime meetings, the seven-person action research team decided on a number of changes to fine-tune the Spalding procedures for the first and third graders and to continue the action research for another year.

Barbara Darroch (2004) had a similar experience while studying elementary math curriculum in graduate school and came up with Singapore Math. She also worked with six teachers, split three and three between the third and fourth grades. She concluded that Singapore Math was responsible for increasing students' Stanford Nine math scores significantly, and the teachers she worked with decided to continue on with the same Singapore Math the next year.

Action researchers also have used the proactive model to test the efficacy of the Accelerated Reader Program for Middle Schoolers (Horn 2004), to establish effective uses of formative evaluation by elementary and secondary faculties to improve instruction (Keech 2004 and Thatcher 2004), to create mentoring to strengthen administrative leadership and staff cohesiveness (Mendoza 2004 and Januzzi 2004), and to develop a statewide network of school business managers to upgrade their knowledge and skills (Grant 2004).

✳ You and Marilyn

Compare yourself with Marilyn Lund.

1. Describe similarities between Marilyn's situation and experiences you have had in your professional career.

2. Justify what you agree with in Marilyn's decisions.

3. Make a supportive argument for what you disagree with in Marilyn's decisions.

4. Apply any of Marilyn's strategies to your own work as an educator.

❈ You and James

Compare yourself with James Johnson.

1. Describe similarities between James's situation and experiences you have had in your professional career.

2. Justify what you agree with in James's decisions.

3. Make a supportive argument for what you disagree with in James's decisions.

4. Apply any of James's strategies to your own work as an educator.

Pilot-Test a Proactive Action Research Project

Step 1: List Hopes and Concerns

Think of a focus for action research you would like to pursue. Try to be explicit about your goals (hopes) for the new practice and be realistic about the obstacles (concerns).

Step 2: Try a New Practice

Decide on a new practice that captures your imagination and inspires you to innovate. Be specific and concrete. Be creative and take a risk.

Step 3: Search for Methods and Collect Data

Now, zero in on the research methods you would use to assess movement toward your hopes. Again, be specific and concrete.

Pilot-Test a Proactive Action Research Project

Step 4: Check on What the Data Mean

Decide on how you will analyze the data. Consider first the students. How can they become involved? Perhaps a colleague or the principal is an appropriate helper. Write down possible candidates and how they can help with the analysis.

Step 5: Reflect on Alternative Ways to Behave

Brainstorm ideas to fine-tune the new practice. Be creative. Find alternative ways to implement the new practice that appeal to you. Discuss those ideas with a critical friend, the students, the principal, and the like. You should be the final judge of how to improve your practice.

Step 6: Fine-Tune the New Practice

Review the data analyses in Steps 3 and 4. Put that together with your Step 5 reflections. Fine-tune your new practice.

Reflections

Reflect on Chapter 5 by answering the following questions:

1. In what ways would proactive action research be useful to you?

2. Create examples of new practices you would like to try because of your reflections, problem solving, reading, discussions with colleagues, or workshops or courses you have attended.

3. Outline three new practices you think would be important to try
   a. In your classroom
   b. In your school
   c. In your district, region, or state

6

Responsive Action Research

A good place to start toward classroom improvement is with facts about the inter-personal situation. A teacher's generalized concern for improvement can become a precise attack on a specific problem as information about the real state of affairs becomes available.

— Robert Fox and Ronald Lippitt (1964)

Teachers, supervisors, and administrators would make better decisions and engage in more effective practices if they were able and willing to conduct research as a basis for these decisions and practices.

—Stephen Corey (1953)

I was introduced to action research as a doctoral student in social psychology at the University of Michigan. Ron Lippitt, my mentor and dissertation chair, demonstrated how action research works in his seminar The Dynamics of Planned Change. His view was that action research is responsive to data because data collection, referred to by Lippitt as "diagnosis," necessarily precedes action.

At that time, teachers could not find much to read about action research, except for a few essays by Kurt Lewin (1948), a monograph by Ron Lippitt (1949), and *Action Research to Improve School Practices* by Stephen Corey (1953). All three authors conceived of action research as alternating cycles of diagnosis and action, with initiation always being diagnosis. In the Lewin tradition, it is assumed that effective "social engineers," whether attorneys, consultants, physicians, psychologists, or teachers, diagnose their clients' problems and the dynamics of their situations before they act.

This model plays out in the experiences of Matt Reardon and Beverly Lee. Both teachers recognized a problem in their classroom, but they collected data from their students before implementing a new practice.

MATT REARDON*

Matt Reardon has taught English to lower-middle-class students at Rosemont High School for five years. He loves to read serious classics, contemporary mysteries, short stories in *Field and Stream*, and essays in *The New Yorker*. He moves easily among William Faulkner, Amanda Cross, Barry Lopez, Marilynne Robinson, Richard Russo, and Jane Smiley and alternates flexibly between novels, poetry, short stories, and expository essays. Matt also writes poetry, and he thinks earnestly of composing a novel about his eight years in the navy. Although he likes to teach, he would rather read or write. Matt teaches to live; he does not live to teach.

In the middle of November, Matt became frustrated with his 12th-grade English literature class. What is happening with this senior class has happened with other senior classes, but it has never been quite this bad. This class is made up of some of the brightest students at Rosemont, but many apparently don't read the assignments. Few students speak up in class when Matt questions them about the readings. He doesn't understand why these 17- and 18-year-olds don't seem to gravitate toward *King Lear*. After all, most have aging grandparents, and most, at least to some extent, have experienced the sibling rivalry of Cordelia, Gonerel, and Regan. Still, they come to class without a clue about the importance of this masterpiece. Instead, they watch the clock and count the minutes until lunch. They're hungry, Matt thinks, but only for food, not great drama, novels, and poetry.

Matt doesn't know how to engage his students. He decides to phone his favorite education professor from college. The two wrote a few letters back and forth when Matt was in the navy, exchange Christmas greetings, and write occasional e-mails since Matt has been teaching, but they haven't had a serious conversation since Matt left college 15 years ago.

In the phone call, Matt presented his frustrations to the professor, who was in her last year of teaching before retirement. The professor listened intently, several times paraphrasing and summarizing Matt's perceptions, and then told Matt that she would mail him an early Christmas present, a book that Matt should read during the Thanksgiving holiday. "It's not a recent book, but it is a classic. I don't remember if I assigned it to you before, but you should read it now. I have extra copies and will mail one to you in the morning," she told him.

In a few days, Matt received a tiny paperback, only 116 pages, with six blank pages in the back for readers to write their reflections and plans. The little book was Herbert Kohl's (1969) precious *The Open Classroom: A Practical Guide to a New Way of Teaching*. Matt had read it when he was in college, but that was a long time ago. Over the four-day holiday, he devoured it. Two final sentences in the section subtitled The Student Underworld reverberated in his mind. "It is essential to listen to the voice of the students. They are not afraid to talk about what actually happens in the school" (pp. 27–28). Matt decided to go directly to his 12th graders on Monday to find out what might help them become more interested in literature.

---

*All names of educators, schools, and communities have been changed.

Matt Collects Data

Matt asks the 12th graders to reflect silently about how his teaching does or does not help them learn English literature. He tells students to print a plus sign on one side of a piece of blank paper and a minus sign on the other. He has them list the helpful things he does on the plus side and the unhelpful things he does on the minus side.

Next, Matt assigns each student to a boy-girl pair. He instructs the pairs to agree on at least two helpful things and two unhelpful things. With 24 students in the class, 12 pairs are formed. Matt asks each pair to meet with another pair and agree on three helpful things and three unhelpful things. He then brings two groups of four together to form groups of eight. Those groups agree on at least four helpful things and four unhelpful things.

Matt tells the students in each eight-person group to count off from 1 to 8; he assigns person number 5 in each of the three groups to act as a spokesperson for his or her group. The three reporters come forward to the front of the room to form a panel. In pooling information from the three eight-person groups, the panel comes up with a total of eight helpful things and ten unhelpful things. (Figure 6.1 lists Matt's helpful and unhelpful teaching techniques.)

Matt thanks the students for their openness and honesty and tells them they will continue to work together with this information next week. When the bell rings, and as the students file out for lunch, three students stop to tell Matt how much they appreciated the day and his sincere effort to improve the class.

Matt Analyzes the Data

During the next few days, Matt looks at the data again and reflects on the themes he sees in them. He thinks that while the students appreciate his expertise in literature

Figure 6.1   Rating Mr. Reardon's Teaching Techniques

Helpful	Unhelpful
Gives information not in the text about authors	Too much lecture
Explains characters well	Covers too many authors
Grades fairly	Assigns too much homework
Shows enthusiasm for literature	Seldom asks us about how we feel or think
Gives extensive feedback on papers	Drills us on what the author's ideas are
Has a good sense of humor	Asks questions that make some of us afraid to make a mistake
Does not favor one sex more than the other	Not enough time spent on difficult assignments (e.g., *King Lear*)
Asks challenging questions	Not enough student-to-student discussion (today is the first time we held discussions in student groups)
	Not always clear about what he wants in our papers
	Sometimes uses words we don't understand

and find his information helpful, they also think he talks too much and doesn't facilitate discussion. In particular, Matt recognizes that his questioning style creates student anxiety and reluctance to speak. Matt wonders about the large number of assignments he gives, and sees that superficial treatment might not be helpful to the students. Matt realizes that the very method he used to obtain these data could be used to get students more involved in discussions about the readings.

On Thursday, Matt tells his students that he wants to use the information they gave him to improve how the class operates. After he summarizes the themes of the data, he asks the students to return to their groups of four and brainstorm actions they would like to see him try.

Matt gives each four-person group a large sheet of blank poster paper with a marker. He tells each group to assign a recorder to print clearly the group's action ideas. After recorders fasten their groups' reports to the wall, students mill around the room to read what the other five groups produced. Next, Matt tells each group to choose three action ideas that they like from the other groups. Matt announces that he will study the action ideas and the students' preferences and give them feedback about the action ideas he'll try.

Matt Uses the Data, Searches for New Ideas, and Announces Changes

The six groups produced a total of 18 action ideas. The class chose six as their favorites. Matt writes those ideas on the chalkboard along with a few comments of his own in parentheses next to each. (See Figure 6.2.)

As Matt feeds the data back to the students and adds his new ideas (information in the parentheses), he sees many students nodding approval. He asks them if he has

Figure 6.2   Six Action Ideas to Improve Mr. Reardon's Class

1. Spend more class time in student groups to learn about the readings. (Use groups of two, four, six, or eight to work on English literature in ways parallel to how we have worked together during the past few days of class.)

2. Students come up with questions to ask Mr. Reardon about authors, their ideas, and literary themes. (Students initiate questions about literature that are important to them, in contrast to me drilling them about the readings. My question to the students: Will you read the assignments if we do that?)

3. Focus on just a few authors; spend more time on each. (Action Ideas 4 and 5 below seem to follow from this idea.)

4. Reread *King Lear* and revisit *Romeo and Juliet*, which we read a while ago, but our study of it was superficial. (Students want to recognize the importance of Shakespeare to English literature, want to understand his plays better, want to relate them to their lives, and a few of them recently found out that Leonard Bernstein's *West Side Story* is patterned after *Romeo and Juliet*.)

5. Read more of Jane Austen's books. (Since Hollywood discovered Jane Austen, students would like to know more about her and her novels.)

6. Students work together to report on readings to one another and to Mr. Reardon. (This action idea is an extension of Idea 1 in this list; it could be integrated with Ideas 2–5 if groups of students were to interview me, for example, about Shakespeare and Jane Austen.)

understood how they want him to improve the class. Virtually all the students chime in with a resounding "Yes!" After searching his mind for relevant literary knowledge, Matt announces the following action ideas to try until the winter holiday break:

> We will reread *King Lear* and *Romeo and Juliet*. Each of you will reread both plays on your own, outside of class. Also, between now and the new calendar year, everyone will watch the videos of Jane Austen's *Pride and Prejudice* (the Laurence Olivier production) and the more recent productions of *Persuasion, Sense and Sensibility,* and *Emma.* You will also be pleased to know that I want you to watch the video of Alicia Silverstone's *Clueless,* because it is a kind of modern version of *Emma.*

> We will work on *King Lear* and *Romeo and Juliet* in small groups. I will assign you to work with different people on each play. We'll start with *King Lear* in groups of four. Tonight, everyone should quickly review the play. I know that it's a long play, but since we've recently studied it, a quick rereading should be sufficient to get us started.

Remembering his course in cooperative learning, Matt then numbers off the four-person groups from one to six. He goes on to say,

> Beginning tomorrow, Groups 1 through 5 will become experts in the acts of the same number of their group. They will prepare reports on the key events and important lines of their group's act. Thus, Group 1 will cover Act 1, Group 2 Act 2, and so forth. Group 6 will have tomorrow to develop questions so that its members can interview me the next day about *King Lear* and Shakespeare. On this coming Friday, we'll discuss how the small groups are working and try to make improvements so that everyone feels good about what he or she is doing.

> On Monday, we'll start with the reports of Groups 1 and 2 on Acts 1 and 2. I'll require each group to report to the whole class, with every member involved in the presentation. We will proceed with Acts 3 and 4 on Tuesday and Act 5 and Group 6's report on the interview on Wednesday. Then we'll see where we are with *King Lear* before going on to *Romeo and Juliet.* By the way, how many of you were in that production of *West Side Story* we did here last spring at Rosemont? [Six students raise their hands.]

Matt's Hopes and Concerns

Matt's hopes are that the students will

- Participate actively with involvement in the small group and whole-class presentations
- Develop favorable attitudes toward the class
- Learn more about literature
- Develop improved skills in writing about literature

Matt's concerns are that some of the students will

- Hitchhike during small-group work and whole-class presentations, depending on others to carry the workload
- Develop uncomfortable feelings toward the class
- Avoid homework reading assignments

Matt Tries a New Practice

Matt carries out the rereading of *King Lear* as planned. He is pleased with how involved most students are with the group work and in making reports to the whole class. Matt notes that those students who have not spoken up in class are now speaking in the small groups and to the whole class. He is impressed with the quality of the group reports and thinks that the interviewers did an adequate job.

For the study of *Romeo and Juliet,* Matt assigns some students to six groups of three each and the rest to one group of six. The group of six comprises students who were in last spring's production of *West Side Story;* Matt has those students report on the similarities and differences between the two plays. Five of the other six groups report on the five acts of *Romeo and Juliet,* while the sixth group reports on an interview with Matt.

After the winter vacation, Matt continues the small-group methods with Jane Austen's novels. He assigns four groups of five each to work on one of Austen's four novels and assigns the fifth group to report on ways in which *Emma* shows up in the movie *Clueless.*

Matt Collects Data

Matt uses three methods to collect data on the students' reactions to the new practices. First, he observes participation and active involvement in the small groups and during whole-class presentations. In particular, Matt is alert to students whose participation is relatively low compared to others. He gives those students extra encouragement. Matt moves from group to group during small-group work to observe and encourage or to answer questions about the reading.

Second, Matt uses part of every Friday's class to interview students about the new practices. He often divides the class into groups of two or three so that all have an opportunity to speak. He sometimes combines groups to engage the students in a whole-group discussion. As a result of these debriefings, Matt is able to fine-tune small-group work as it progresses.

Third, Matt asks a colleague, Bob Harsted, to join the class as it reports about *Romeo and Juliet.* Bob teaches music, and he directed Rosemont's production of *West Side Story.* As the presentations proceed, Bob gives feedback to Matt and to the class about what he observes. The six-person group that was part of the *West Side Story* production invites Bob to participate in its presentation to the class. After class, Matt and Bob chat about ways to get students excited about literature, theater, and music.

The following spring, Matt converts the list of helpful and unhelpful teaching techniques into a structured questionnaire. (See Figure 6.3 for the questionnaire.)

With this questionnaire, Matt assesses the merit of his new practices. He sees if students agree that he has continued the helpful techniques and discontinued the unhelpful techniques. To assess the worth of his practices, Matt develops an essay exam similar to ones he has used before and judges how well this class of 12th

Figure 6.3   Perceptions of How Our Class Operates

Below is a list of 18 things that could happen in our class. Please circle one answer next to each item to show whether you strongly agree, agree, feel neutral, disagree, or strongly disagree (SA, A, N, D, SD). In this class, Mr. Reardon

1. Gives information not in the text about authors

    SA   A   N   D   SD

2. Lectures too much

    SA   A   N   D   SD

3. Explains characters well

    SA   A   N   D   SD

4. Covers too many authors

    SA   A   N   D   SD

5. Is fair in grading

    SA   A   N   D   SD

6. Assigns too much homework

    SA   A   N   D   SD

7. Shows enthusiasm for literature

    SA   A   N   D   SD

8. Seldom asks us about what we feel or think

    SA   A   N   D   SD

9. Gives extensive feedback on papers

    SA   A   N   D   SD

10. Drills us on what the authors are trying to get across

    SA   A   N   D   SD

11. Has a good sense of humor

    SA   A   N   D   SD

12. Questions us in ways that make us afraid to make a mistake

    SA   A   N   D   SD

13. Does not favor one sex more than the other

    SA   A   N   D   SD

14. Does not spend enough time on difficult assignments

    SA   A   N   D   SD

15. Asks challenging questions

    SA   A   N   D   SD

16. Does not have enough student-to-student discussion

    SA   A   N   D   SD

17. Is not clear about what he wants in our papers

    SA   A   N   D   SD

18. Uses words we don't understand

    SA   A   N   D   SD

graders compares to others. The data show significant improvement in students' attitudes about the class and what they are learning, and improvement in their skills in writing. But there are still a few problems. With these results, he feels ready to announce new action ideas that he'll try for the rest of the academic year. He decides to make responsive action research a regular part of teaching 12th graders. He'll consider it for other classes.

BEVERLY LEE*

After her freshman year in college, Beverly married and lived around the world because of her husband's position in the air force. While they were stationed in England, Beverly attended group relations conferences at the Tavistock Institute of Human Relations. There she learned about Jacob Moreno's (1953) ideas about the power of peer groups in child development. At age 39, Beverly began work on a BA in elementary education and a teaching certificate. After graduation, she was unable to obtain a regular teaching position, so she became a substitute teacher for two years and worked in six districts. She substituted mostly in elementary schools with upper-middle-class families. Last August, she got a job teaching fourth graders at McQueen Elementary School. McQueen is a K–5 school, serving a racially and ethnically diverse population of blue-collar and unemployed families.

After her first month of teaching, Beverly is surprised by a number of things about her 27 fourth graders at McQueen. She is pleasantly surprised to find that

- All students can read at least at a second-grade level.
- The students are seldom absent or tardy.
- Quite a number of parents have visited the school.
- She relates well to all students regardless of their race, ethnicity, or sex.

She is unpleasantly surprised by how rarely she sees the students of different races play or work together. The students of each racial group usually stick together. Although she hasn't seen intergroup bickering or fighting, she observes that members of the different racial groups don't volunteer to work together on schoolwork unless she requires them to do so. The few times Beverly required members of different racial groups to work together on a project, the students ended up working by themselves.

In doing a methods search, Beverly remembers what she learned at Tavistock and digs out college notes about how to measure social relationships in elementary classrooms. She finds a sociometric questionnaire titled How I Feel About Others in My Class. (See Figure 6.4 for the questionnaire.) She decides to give it a try.

Beverly Collects Data

Beverly duplicates an alphabetical list of class members and numbers them from 1 to 27. She gives the class roster and a copy of the questionnaire to each student. She asks the students to complete the questionnaire. She explains that she wants to

---

*All names of educators, schools, and communities have been changed.

Figure 6.4   *How I Feel About Others in My Class*

Everybody has different feelings about everybody else. We like some people, we don't know others well, and we would like to get to know some people better. If the teacher knows the way you really feel about other members of your class, he or she can often plan things better. There are no right or wrong answers. (Use the class list to answer the following questions.)

Which three students in this class do you like the most?   Student's number
_____
_____
_____

Which three students in this class do you know least well?   Student's number
_____
_____
_____

Which three students in this class would you like to know better?   Student's number
_____
_____
_____

Adapted from *Group Processes in the Classroom*, 8th ed. (Schmuck and Schmuck 2001:138). Reprinted with permission from McGraw-Hill Companies, Inc.

establish a climate in which everyone feels friendly toward everyone else and where students can give her ideas about how to make the class more cohesive.

Beverly Analyzes the Data

Beverly finds that students of each racial group select students from their own racial groups when answering the first question on the questionnaire. In every case, a boy and a girl emerge as sociometric stars (chosen frequently) in each racial group. Thus she finds six students (three girls and three boys) who are well liked by about one-third of the students in the class. Beverly has lunch with those six students and asks them if they will help her analyze data from the questionnaire. She tells the class about the six students who will help her work on the data and assures the class that all students will get the opportunity to work with Beverly on this project.

When the six students meet with Beverly, she shows them a large matrix for the data analysis. On the left side of the matrix, she has a vertical list of numbers from 1 to 27. Across the top of the matrix, she prints the letters L, O, and B. The L stands for liking choices, O stands for know-least-well choices, and B stands for like-to-know-better choices.

Beverly asks two African American students to fill out the L column, two European Americans to fill out the O column, and two Native Americans to fill out the B column. She cuts up the completed questionnaires into three parts and gives each pair the sections it needs to do its tallying. After the data are arrayed, Beverly asks the six students to form an all-girls' group and an all-boys' group to discuss the following:

1. Which students do our classmates know least well? What kinds of things do they have in common?

2. Which students do our classmates want to know better? What kinds of things do they have in common?

3. What students, including the six of you, are chosen as most liked? What kinds of things do you and they have in common?

4. What ideas do you have for how we can get to know everybody better in our class?

Several themes emerge from the discussions of the two student groups.

First, students we know least well are newest to the class, quiet, or shy, and are more often boys than girls. Second, students we want to know better are in all of the racial groups, are a little more outgoing and social compared to those in the least-well-known group, and are more often girls than boys. Third, most-liked students are like us, outgoing and social, and from both sexes and different racial groups.

When Beverly probes for the discussion groups' action ideas, a fourth and fifth theme emerge. The students say, "We who are liked by others should work more with the least-well-known students, and the whole class should try to find things that we all have in common."

Beverly Distributes the Data, Searches for Knowledge, and Announces Changes

Beverly asks the six students to feed back the sociometric data to their classmates. First, each pair reports what it tallied in each of the three columns. Second, the group of girls and the group of boys each reports on themes and action ideas. The girls report on the first theme, and the boys report on the second theme. Beverly tells the class about the third theme. Then the girls report on the fourth theme: people in the L column working more with people in the O column. The boys report on the fifth theme: the whole class working to find things that all students have in common.

After rereading her notes from the group relations conferences at Tavistock, Beverly studies Chapter 5 titled "Friendship and Class Cohesiveness" in the text she read as part of an inservice workshop in her school (Schmuck and Schmuck 2001). She decides to start four activities the following week:

1. Learning about being a friend

2. Making a class book about friends

3. Finding commonalities and strengths

4. Reading trios to increase understanding of one another

Beverly Reports Her Hopes and Tries a New Practice

The next day, Beverly tells her students that she hopes everyone will become more friendly with one another during the next month. She says that she hopes that having friends will result in improved academic learning and a safer, more secure and relaxed class climate.

She tells the class members they will work together for 45 minutes every day to develop friendliness among classmates. She announces that the first activity is to learn about what it means to be a friend. She starts this activity by pairing up the students with one group of three. She forms the pairs as follows:

- Students of different racial groups
- Highly liked students with least-well-known students
- Students the class wants to know better

Beverly asks each pair to think of two friendly behaviors and two unfriendly behaviors. Next, she asks the pairs to form into groups of four and the group of three to remain a group. She asks the groups to agree on three important friendly behaviors and three important unfriendly behaviors. Next, Beverly asks each four-person group and the three-person group to report to the whole class. Each individual reports on at least one important behavior from his or her small group. Beverly prints the ideas on large sheets of poster paper in front of the class. She leads the whole class in a discussion to generate lists of ten friendly behaviors and ten unfriendly behaviors. Later, Beverly prints the two lists neatly on large cardboard posters to display on the classroom walls.

A few days later, Beverly starts the second activity: a class book about friends. In the initial phase, racially heterogeneous groups of three come up with sayings about friendship. For example, one trio came up with "You can be yourself with your friends." Another trio came up with "Friends are there when you need them." Next, each trio draws a picture to illustrate its saying. Beverly puts the sayings and illustrations into a class book. Later, she forms students into racially heterogeneous groups of five (with two groups of six) to make lists of characteristics of their friends. She also prints those characteristics in the class book. She then assigns racially heterogeneous pairs (with one group of three) to create a story about friends. She prints those stories in the class book as well. At an open house, students show their parents those parts of the class book they created.

Beverly carries out two more activities. For the first activity, students work in small, racially mixed groups to come up with commonalities in the class. They also brainstorm strengths of individual students. For the second activity, she brings racially mixed trios to the "reading corner," where they read with her. She works with the reading trios while other students read silently, do computer projects, or receive special tutoring from middle school students.

Beverly Collects Data

Beverly uses three research methods to assess how effective the new practices are. First, she observes communication between members of the different racial groups. She watches during formal class sessions, informal moments between formal activities, and at recess, at lunch, and after school.

Second, Beverly eats lunch once a month with different groups of five or six. She thinks of these gatherings as focus group interviews, during which she asks students for their perceptions and feelings about cross-racial friendships in the class.

Third, Beverly invites middle school students, themselves racially diverse, to her classroom to interview them about how they view intergroup relations in her class. She also asks them for ideas for improving the situation.

Figure 6.5 How I Interact With My Classmates

Please rate your 27 classmates on the following activities:

Working together in a small group (circle one):

| Yes, for sure | Yes | Neutral | No |

Playing games together outside the class (circle one):

| Yes, for sure | Yes | Neutral | No |

Read together with the teacher (circle one):

| Yes, for sure | Yes | Neutral | No |

Attending a class party together (circle one):

| Yes, for sure | Yes | Neutral | No |

Writing together in class (circle one):

| Yes, for sure | Yes | Neutral | No |

Beverly uses another sociometric method, the Roster-and-Rating Questionnaire (Schmuck and Schmuck 2001), to assess progress toward the goal of a more friendly, supportive, and cohesive fourth-grade class. (See Figure 6.5 for the questionnaire.) She gives the students a list of all 27 classmates, asking them to rate the degree to which they would like to work or play with each classmate. She provides a 4-point scale.

Beverly also asks each student to write a two-page essay about five peers in the class with whom they have developed a friendship during the school year. The essay should include the reasons why the author believes his or her feelings have become more friendly toward those five peers.

Beverly wants to find out whether the progress she perceives is corroborated by the students' subjective responses. She also wants to see whether students' two-page essays help her get new insights into how friendships were formed in this class. This might give her new ideas about how to integrate friendship formation into academic learning.

Beverly is pleased with the results. Many new friendships have formed, and every student is now known well by others. She is especially pleased with the many cross-race friendships that have formed in the class and how well students cooperate with one another on academic learning. She will continue to spend 45 minutes a week on building class cohesiveness and improving race relations.

THE SIX STEPS OF RESPONSIVE ACTION RESEARCH

Since lack of information or a desire to make a diagnosis represents the starting point of the responsive model, reflect on things you would like to know about your students' perceptions, attitudes, and behaviors. What sorts of data do you want to obtain from the class you're targeting? Next, do a formal methods search. Go to the search engines on your computer. Go to the book chapters cited in Chapter 5 when Step 3 (Search for Methods and Collect Data) is described. Review the 25 instruments in Schmuck and Schmuck (2001). Zero in on a few methods to collect data that will be useful to you. Then proceed.

Figure 6.6   Six Steps of Responsive Action Research

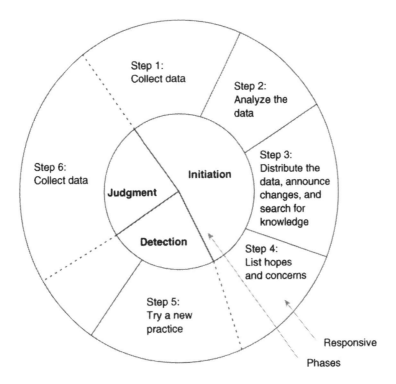

Slower to move to a new practice than its proactive counterpart, responsive research's first four steps constitute initiation. This phase incorporates four practices new to students:

1. Teachers ask students for ideas on improving the class.

2. Teachers engage students as partners in data interpretation.

3. Teachers feed back the students' data with their own interpretations of the data and search for knowledge about new practices.

4. Teachers decide on their hopes and concerns for the new practices they intend to try.

Although Step 5 is implementation and detection and Step 6 entails judgment, both detection and judgment also occur as part of Steps 1–4. Responsive action research, simply stated, entails diagnosis, action, and evaluation. Figure 6.6 illustrates the connection between the steps and phases of responsive action research.

Step 1: Collect Data

On the threshold of initiating responsive action research, you sense that your teaching could improve and a few classroom events could be designed differently. Although ambivalent about soliciting critical feedback from students, doing so permits more effectiveness in teaching. Collect objective data about students' thoughts and feelings and initiate a constructive strategy to improve current classroom interaction patterns.

The initial data collection is short and simple. It can be as straightforward as

- Matt Reardon's plus and minus signs on two sides of blank paper
- Pairs of students discussing strengths and weaknesses of teaching methods
- Students picking four peers to work with on a project
- A simple sentence completion inventory
- An open-ended "Who am I?" questionnaire
- A sociometric questionnaire
- A colleague's observation
- Audiotaping a classroom discussion with students

Collect data from students in a public and official manner to communicate the importance of the endeavor. It is crucial to convey to everyone in class that the data will be used to bring about improvement.

Step 2: Analyze the Data

Analyze the data to find recurrent themes and patterns. The analysis can be done alone, as Matt did, or with a small group of students, as Beverly did. A colleague, or the whole class, can also help analyze the data.

An important aspect of data analysis is finding ideas for action. While the themes or patterns depict how students think and feel about current classroom interactions, action ideas represent instrumental strategies for moving from the current situation to a more ideal place. The combination of themes and action ideas generates creative new practices. For example, Matt realized that students could question him instead of him questioning them. Beverly discovered the power of racially mixed student groups working together on a project.

Searching for themes and action ideas opens a window to the present and maps the future. Do not become overly preoccupied with whether the data are valid and reliable. Remember, internal validity rather than external validity is your main concern. If the themes and action ideas have the ring of truth to you, you're on the right track. Strive for precision with this specific group of students. Satisfy yourself that the data are helpful and that the new actions feel right.

Step 3: Distribute the Data, Announce Changes, and Search for Knowledge

Select a limited number of themes and action ideas. Do not attempt to cover all the data or all the possible actions that you could take. The key to this step is to show a logical connection between what you learn from the data and the changes you implement. State to the class what specific changes you will try during the next few weeks or months. This presents students with a road map of future classroom interaction, reasserts the seriousness of the changes, and offers a contract to which teacher and students are accountable. The announcement, however, should not cause a continuance of new practices that turn out poorly.

Step 4: List Hopes and Concerns

Now, become explicit about your hopes by using verbal constructions like *to develop, to achieve, to reach, to produce, to facilitate,* and so on. And give special attention to concerns or obstacles that might keep your hopes from being reached.

Step 5: Try a New Practice

Implement practices that are new to you and to the students. Give the new practice at least two months to take shape and have an effect. Do not invite colleagues or the principal to observe the innovation too soon, unless they were collaborating with you from the start. Allow several success experiences before formal evaluations. Fine-tune along the way and make needed modifications as challenges arise. Reflect on the present, but stay the course.

Step 6: Collect Data

While you're implementing the new practice, remain vigilant to yourself and to your students' reactions. This is the time to reflect on the present. Remain sensitive to the present flow of classroom interaction, to expressions of feelings, to approach and avoidance behaviors, and to ways the class does or does not cooperate as a group.

Check on how others react through unstructured observation. Watch specifically for smiles and laughter, for heads nodding in agreement, for eye-to-eye connections, for heads bent toward one another, and for the ease with which students approach you and one another. Try structured observation by counting rates of talking, by listening for paraphrasing, summarizing, and feeling statements, and by tuning in to the frequency of statements that use words such as *we, us, our group,* and *our class.*

Interview students about their perceptions and feelings. Matt did this when he interviewed students about their group work in English literature during his Friday debriefings. Beverly did it when she interviewed six different students at a time and invited the middle school students to her classroom. Think about how to interview individual students, small student groups, and the whole class about their reactions to the new practices.

After the new practice has been tried for an extended period, there are three reasons to collect additional data:

1. To assess whether the new practice has merit (Are the students satisfied with the practice? Have they developed more positive attitudes? Do they show more appreciation for one another and for the curriculum?)

2. To judge whether the new practice has worth (Are the students learning the curriculum as hoped? Do they behave differently toward one another and toward you? Do the students perform better on academic tasks? Are there things they can do now that they can take with them next year?)

3. To uncover new themes or action ideas that emerged while the new practice was implemented (Are there any unexpected gains from the new practices? Are there any unintended negative consequences from the practice?)

Now look for a new focus for the next cycle of action research. You are fully engaged in continuous improvement.

THE RANGE OF RESPONSIVE MODELS

The responsive model can be applied to many educational problems at different levels and in diverse contexts.

Matt Reardon, a high school literature teacher, knew that his students were not learning to appreciate the classics and that they were not writing about them very intelligently, but he didn't know exactly what to do. Since he had been teaching his students for a few months, he thought: Why not ask them about how to make the class better?

Beverly Lee believed that her fourth graders would learn to read and do math better if they could become more friendly and supportive of one another. She thought: Why not engage them in action research so that they could look at data together about their interpersonal relationships? Perhaps while doing action research collaboratively, Beverly's students would come up with some new ways to improve their social-emotional climate so that together they would read and do math better.

I should add that along with Matt and Beverly, middle school teachers too should consider the power of the responsive model for their students. In particular, 13-, 14-, and 15-year-olds seek to become actively involved in making their school experiences more engaging and interesting. They would enjoy collecting, analyzing, and using data to take new action.

Sherilynn Boehlert, principal of Ketchikan (Alaska) Charter School, was concerned that parent participation had declined precipitously during the last two years. She engaged Ketchikan's Academic Policy Committee (APC), its governing board, in discussions to reflect on the drop in parent involvement.

Together the APC raised the questions: How can parental involvement be increased at APC meetings, and how can we work better toward our goal of all families meeting Ketchikan's original Participation and Volunteer Agreement? With Boehlert's help, the APC decided to use the responsive model to collect data from the parents of Ketchikan's students.

Using quantitative and qualitative methods, the APC collected questionnaire and interview data on the parents' attitudes toward APC meetings, other parent gatherings—such as open houses and parent-teacher conferences—and about the original agreement.

To analyze the data, the APC formed a new Program Enhancement Committee (PEC) with a few APC members for overlap and additional parents and teachers who were not APC members. The PEC analyzed the action research data, listed its hopes and concerns for positive change, and held problem-solving discussions about new actions to take.

Although more parents became involved during the last few months of that school year, the PEC decided to continue the project by collecting another round of data, especially targeting parents who did not contribute data in the first round.

Read Boehlert (2004) for fascinating details about the data collection instruments, specific analysis procedures used by the PEC, and actions that the PEC initiated to increase parental involvement at Ketchikan.

In a very different example of the responsive model, Debra Slagle turned an inadequate school into an adequate school in two years. In early 2002, Westwind Preparatory Academy was categorized as "underperforming" by the Arizona Department of Education. Immediately Slagel introduced her faculty to responsive action research, amassed three years of student test data on the Arizona Instrument to Measure Standards (AIMS), and initiated a structured plan for the faculty to analyze the test data and to take constructive action to improve its teaching and the students' learning.

Slagle's plan called for the faculty to work in small subject-matter groups to

- Pinpoint areas of greatest student underperformance on the AIMS
- Create a list of causes for the lack of student performance on the AIMS
- Act in new ways to increase student performance on the AIMS
- Assign specific actions to every faculty member so that they would all be accountable for student performance on the AIMS

By late 2003, Westwind students showed significant improvement in reading, writing, and math. By 2004, they were doing even better in reading and math. Read Slagle (2004) for a moving story about how a small high school reinvented itself and about Westwind's next steps in action research.

Although most projects that use the responsive model focus on classroom or school problems, the range can go beyond them. Take, for example, the case of a school board collecting data from the citizens of Hamilton in Chapter 8. There we have an example of an educator-stakeholder task force executing a communitywide responsive project.

An excellent example of another project that lies outside classrooms and the school is Marta Reyes's action research to reinvent the California Network of Educational Charters (CANEC). As CANEC's new president in 2002, Reyes took the opportunity to lead the then ten-year-old network through responsive action research to reinvigorate it and raise it to a new level of effectiveness.

Using data from three questionnaires and a collaborative analysis procedure, Reyes led CANEC's board through the steps of the responsive model. Read Reyes (2004) for her well-articulated, vivid details of each step and for a description of how the board dealt with unexpected setbacks in creating the new California Charter Schools Association (CCSA), which Reyes says "offers even more opportunities for both proactive and responsive action research" (p. 64).

❇ You and Matt

Compare yourself with Matt Reardon.

1. Describe similarities between Matt's situation and your experiences in your professional career.

2. Justify what you agree with in Matt's decisions.

3. Make a supportive argument for what you disagree with in Matt's decisions.

4. Apply any of Matt's strategies to your own work as an educator.

❈ You and Beverly

Compare yourself with Beverly Lee.

1. Describe the similarities between Beverly's situation and your professional career.

2. Justify what you agree with in Beverly's decisions.

3. Make a supportive argument for what you disagree with in Beverly's decisions.

4. Apply any of Beverly's strategies to your own work as an educator.

Pilot-Test a Responsive Action Research Project

Step 1: Collect Data

List data collection methods you might use. Think of questionnaires, interviews, observations, and documents. Perhaps a needs assessment is in order. Try to be concrete and specific.

Step 2: Analyze the Data

List those who might assist with the analysis. Seek to involve students in tallying and organizing the data. Are there colleagues, administrators, or parents who might help? Initiate collaboration with others to make the data more valid and reliable.

Step 3: Distribute the Data, Announce Changes, and Search for Knowledge

Think of your audiences to receive data feedback. Design a sequence of feedback sessions. Create logical connections between the data and changes you wish to try. Search for knowledge about the changes; use library and computer resources.

✻ Pilot-Test a Responsive Action Research Project

Step 4: List Hopes and Concerns

Be explicit and specific about your hopes and concerns for the changes you will make.

Step 5: Try a New Practice

Design the new practice. Create a rough timeline and do your best to stick with it, but do not become a slave to the clock. During the first few weeks of using the new practice, fine-tune as you go. Concentrate on reflecting on the present.

Step 6: Collect Data

Divide this step into two parts. First, check daily on how the students are reacting to the new practice. Focus data collections on informal student interviews and observant participation. Ask students to serve as formal observers. Second, seek to assess the merit and worth of the new practice. Reflect on the methods that worked best in Step 1. Strive to measure outcomes.

❇ Reflections

Reflect on Chapter 6 by answering the following questions:

1. In what ways would responsive action research be useful to you?

2. Create examples of research methods that you would feel comfortable using.

3. Brainstorm data collection procedures that you might use in the following three settings:

   1. In your classroom

   2. In your school

   3. In your district, region, or state

7

Group Dynamics of Cooperative Action Research

Teachers cannot create and sustain the conditions for the productive development of children if those conditions do not exist for teachers.

—Seymour Sarason (1990)

Action research . . . is noncompetitive and nonexploitative and enhances the lives of all participants. This collaborative approach to inquiry seeks to build positive working relationships.

—Ernest T. Stringer (1996)

Sarason (1990) reminds administrators and policy makers that teachers need to engage in personal development as much as their students. Even though teachers assume the role of responsible adults, they still are developing human beings. He argues that teachers need nurturance and support for their professional development just as much as students do for their self-esteem and academic learning.

Australian educator Ernest Stringer (1996) helped workers perform community-based action research in a variety of community and organizational settings. Stringer's community-based action research is analogous to cooperative action research in schools, in which teachers work together to reach goals important to all of them. Stringer argued that community-based action research is successful when participants work together with honesty, nondefensiveness, openness, and a spirit of cooperation and equality.

Cooperative school-based action research establishes positive work relationships among administrators, teachers, specialists, classified staff members, parents, board members, and students. Along with skills of reflection and problem solving, knowledge of research methods, and an understanding of steps and phases of proactive or responsive action research, cooperative action research requires group dynamics skills.

School participants with common concerns and interests use cooperative action research to inquire about educational issues. The word *cooperative* refers to joint work to reach the same end, while the word *collaborative* refers to joint work to promote individual ends. Thus examples of action research in Chapter 8 are cooperative, while instances of mutual work, portrayed in Chapters 5 and 6, are collaborative. Three types of group dynamics characterize effective cooperative action research: positive social support, critical friendship, and probing conversation.

POSITIVE SOCIAL SUPPORT

Positive social support requires team members to communicate esteem, respect, and mutual obligation to one another. Figure 7.1 lists some important traits of supportive communication.

Positive social support enhances the ability of team members to feel secure and to perform competently. For instance, soldiers perform dangerous duties more effectively when interpersonal relations in their platoons are friendly and supportive. Industrial work groups perform more successfully when interdependent workers communicate mutual respect for one another. Participants' ideas in problem-solving groups are accepted and used more when they are friendly with one another. Students achieve better academically when they feel accepted and respected by their classmates (Schmuck and Schmuck 2001).

When people cooperate in groups, they frequently feel anxiety about how they will perform. They think: "Will I be competent here? Will I be able to contribute to this group's success? Who will appreciate me in this group? Will they think I am carrying my load? Will people listen to my ideas? How can I exert my will here?" These questions reveal human beings' deep concerns about competence, acceptance, and influence.

Three psychological needs should be met with positive social support: achievement, affiliation, and power. Supportive communication within cohesive groups enhances participants' self-esteem by satisfying those needs. The need for achievement is satisfied by joining together to solve important challenges. The affiliation

Figure 7.1   Traits of Supportive Communication

Supportive communication includes

- Understanding others' ideas and feelings
- Acknowledging others' beliefs and values
- Showing concern for others' welfare and happiness
- Giving help and acknowledging obligation
- Expressing empathy and positive feelings

need is satisfied by expressing positive feelings, help, and obligation to one another. The power need is satisfied by acknowledging the importance of one another's ideas and feelings as they work together. Without a strong foundation of positive social support, cooperative action research will not succeed.

CRITICAL FRIENDSHIP

Constructive criticism exchanged between friends helps convert anxiety into positive energy. Since teachers perform most daily routines without much adult interaction, they need to learn how to exchange constructive criticism and how to act as critical friends with colleagues.

In graduate seminars with highly seasoned administrators and teachers, I often ask pairs of critical friends to exchange feedback about their essays on educational leadership and research before turning them in. Using critical friendship as a teaching device is helpful because most experienced adult K–12 educators feel insecure about their ability to write competent essays, research reports, master's theses, and doctoral dissertations. Pairing students often helps them cope with their fear of failure in writing. (See Figure 7.2 for a list of my collaborative peer-tutoring steps.)

Critical friendship pairs do best when preceded by team building and cooperative learning. Participants pick their partners and initially meet with an instructor for input, guidance, and support. Encourage pairs to recognize common ground and to understand assumptions that undergird critical friendship (see Figure 7.3).

Critical friendships can enhance effectiveness of both individual and cooperative action research. An example of working collaboratively is Marilyn Lund and the fifth-grade teacher from another school who used critical friendship to

Figure 7.2 Collaborative Peer-Tutoring Steps

In the style of two-way, collaborative peer tutoring, participants work through the following steps with each other:

1. Each participant writes a 500-word draft about an educational issue he or she would like to research.

2. The partners exchange their drafts for an initial reading.

3. Without referring to the draft, each writer explains to his or her partner the main points to be made in the essay.

4. Each listener (tutor) gives feedback to the writer about gaps between the essay and the oral summary. This helps each writer see how his or her draft could be written more clearly.

5. The partners tell each other how they will rewrite their essays.

6. Each partner reads the other's draft, circling anything that is unclear, inaccurate, grammatically incorrect, and so on. This helps each writer become more precise in his or her prose.

7. Each student spends time alone to rewrite the draft.

8. The partners either hand in the essay or exchange the second draft with their partner for additional constructive criticism.

Figure 7.3 Assumptions That Undergird the Critical Friendship Procedure

- Positive social support alone does not facilitate learning, development, or problem solving. Critical feedback about shortcomings must accompany positive social support, allowing the recipient to correct mistakes, reduce errors, and improve his or her understanding.
- People accept and use criticism more enthusiastically when it comes from an empathic peer rather than an impersonal source.
- Positive social support and constructive criticism facilitate learning when they are delivered within the social framework of an egalitarian and reciprocally helpful relationship.

critique each other's projects. Another example is two teams of action researchers, each doing their own cooperative action research, who use critical friendship to critique one another's projects. A single team also uses critical friendship on itself when it stands back from doing business to critique its own project. Positive social support and critical friendship are essential to the success of cooperative action research.

PROBING CONVERSATION

Probing conversations occur between critical friends in one-on-one interviews or within or between teams in focus group interviews. Like exchanges between critical friends, probing conversations entail mutual help and reciprocal obligation between egalitarian partners. Probing conversations go beyond the usual content of interviews between critical friends to focus on larger school issues.

Probing conversations among educators usually take place during faculty meetings, within grade-level teams, at departmental gatherings, during site council or special task force meetings, or at staff retreats and inservice workshops. Conversations between new partners typically last for 90 minutes. Each individual or team has an opportunity to talk for 45 minutes about significant outcomes they believe can be affected by changing school practices.

During probing conversations, individual or group participants strive to mirror their partners' perceptions by frequently paraphrasing and summarizing their partners' statements. The interviewers confront the others' reflections by probing for clarity and specificity. The conversation deepens each participant's concerns about effective teaching and learning.

Since probing conversations rarely occur among teachers in the same school, have the collaborating or cooperating partners (individuals or teams) meet privately with each other in special places at special times. At initial gatherings, do not expect the pairs to report to others about their conversations. Later, after action research becomes a way of school life, probing conversations about teaching and learning will occur in public forums. At that time, administrators or teachers might present their action research designs to site councils or special task forces while teams report on their cooperative plans to the whole staff. Indeed, public presentations enhance the power of school action research. The deep reflection, open conversation, and planning required to create a coherent public presentation serve as impetus for team members to coalesce their ideas and give extra cooperative energy to the project. Making public presentations together also facilitates team cohesiveness. Figure 7.4 is an example of a probing conversation.

Figure 7.4   A Probing Conversation

After attending a conference on teacher research, four young teachers from the same middle school decide to work together on some sort of research project. They report this interest to their principal, who says she will support their effort. The principal asks a seasoned teacher to take the role of facilitator and engage the research team in a probing conversation.

FACILITATOR: Let's start with the four of you brainstorming issues in the school—particularly problems in teaching and learning—that you have been reflecting on lately.

TEACHERS:

- Students don't show respect toward our special-needs youngsters.
- Our faculty is not very cohesive.
- Our social studies curriculum is textbook dominated.
- Too many students are lackadaisical about schoolwork.
- Our students have a love-hate relationship with the businesses in the area.
- Middle school students are confused about who they are and where they are going.

FACILITATOR: Tell me more about the problems.

TEACHERS: [The teachers elaborate.]

FACILITATOR: OK, good. I heard you refer to six different problems. Let me try to paraphrase each one. [The facilitator paraphrases the list of six.] Am I accurate?

TEACHERS: Yes.

FACILITATOR: Now, talk about ways in which you think the six problems might be interrelated.

TEACHERS:

- Early adolescence is a period of confusion.
- Confused identities are what the students experience.
- School doesn't engage their interests.
- Many of our colleagues are burned out trying to teach these kids.
- Teachers are trying to build a life away from the job to keep their sanity.
- We expect students to sit and listen for too much time.

FACILITATOR: Can you give me some examples?

TEACHERS: [The teachers give specific examples.]

FACILITATOR: Let me summarize what I think the problems are in teaching and learning that concern you the most: kids of this age are active yet confused. They are difficult to work with in the traditional school culture. Teachers get worn out trying to motivate the students; they prefer to stay away from the kids as much as possible. It strikes me that both the students and the teachers need activities or events to raise their spirits. Am I accurate?

TEACHERS:

- You're on to something; yes, the students and the teachers both seem to want to avoid each other.
- I like your phrase "raise their spirits"; this is a school without much spirit.
- Yes, we should try something new to cut through this lack of spirit.
- Perhaps we could do something with school spirit or with our dull social studies curriculum.

FACILITATOR: Now, let me see if I understand how you see the current situation. There is rather low morale all around with the students and the teachers. Students and teachers alike are lackadaisical about schoolwork. Correct?

TEACHERS: Right on!

FACILITATOR: And let me see if I understand how you see the ideal targets you wish to strive toward. You want a school culture in which everyone is enthusiastic about teaching and learning together. Am I accurate?

(Continued)

Figure 7.4 (Continued)

TEACHERS: Yes, indeed you are.

FACILITATOR: OK, let's brainstorm the helping and hindering forces you see in the situation. What is helping you move toward your target?

TEACHERS:

- A supportive principal
- A modern facility
- Supportive parents
- Some area businesses that support our students
- A few teachers who will try something innovative
- Some students who are enthusiastic about the school

FACILITATOR: What is keeping you from moving toward your target?

TEACHERS:

- Many worn-out veteran teachers
- The development stage of students
- Textbook-dominated curriculum
- Outdated faculty philosophy on proper teaching
- Rejection of our students by some businesses

FACILITATOR: Now let's brainstorm together about new actions you might take to reduce the hindering forces and increase the helping forces.

TEACHERS:

- Throw out the text in social studies.
- Organize small groups of students to cooperate in community service projects.
- Get interested faculty to join us in a social studies program of community service projects.

FACILITATOR: Let's brainstorm about research data you might collect to see how others in the school community relate to the problem.

TEACHERS:

- Questionnaire for students about the social studies curriculum
- Interview with our colleagues about ways to improve teacher and student morale
- Interview with businesspeople in the area
- Library research on community service projects in middle schools
- Observations in a few social studies classes that get high ratings from the students

FACILITATOR: I hope I've helped you get a running start on your cooperative action research project.

EFFECTIVE GROUP DYNAMICS

Successful cooperative action research requires participants' competence in four domains: reflection, problem solving, research methods, and group dynamics.

Excellence in the first three does not compensate for deficiencies in the last. For cooperative action research to work well, it requires effective group dynamics.

Ten Tips for Group Dynamics

Following are tips about group dynamics to keep in mind.

Tip 1: Establish Feelings of Membership, Inclusion, and Trust

Participants must feel secure in their group membership. Secure membership means that members of the action research team feel confident that other members want them to be integral group members. Spend time helping every member learn a few personal things about every other member. Feelings of inclusion pave the way for development of interpersonal trust whereby members feel secure to be themselves and do not feel threatened to disagree or hold different points of view.

Tip 2: Foster Shared Influence and Dispersed Leadership

All participants should believe they can affect what the group does. Shared influence means that each member contributes important content to the action research design and that each individual's contributions dovetail with other members' contributions. Dispersed leadership similarly means that everyone rotates task and social-emotional roles in a reciprocal fashion to help the group carry out steps and phases of action research.

Tip 3: Accentuate Friendliness and Cohesiveness

Although members of an action research team do not need to be friends, cooperation is smoother if participants express friendly feelings toward one another by performing social-emotional functions during group work. Social-emotional functions include being warm and responsive to others, sensing feeling and mood within the group, attempting to reconcile disagreements, seeing that others have a chance to speak, and expressing standards that will help a group remain cohesive.

Friendliness is enhanced when everyone values a few important things about everyone else and has insights and knowledge about every other member. Cohesiveness means that group members identify themselves as a team and that they pull together to support one another in carrying out action research.

Tip 4: Cope With Social Status Differences

When action research teams comprise teachers, administrators, classified staff members, students, parents, board members, or citizens at large, significant social status differences among members are inevitable. In such diverse groups, members whose status is lower than others often participate less and feel left out. Care must be taken to ensure that every member, regardless of status, is treated with the same attention and respect as every other member.

Tip 5: Use Sound Meeting Skills

The group should use sound meeting skills to see that every member's ideas and skills are used to plan and execute the action research. A convener and a recorder should facilitate team meetings. Conveners have authority to move the group through tasks, bring silent members into discussion, and remain vigilant in getting the group through its agenda. Recorders help conveners keep the group on task by writing down important group decisions and, from time to time, by summarizing group decisions during the meeting. As the team matures, roles of convener and recorder can be rotated through the membership. The following meeting skills are useful tools to keep the group focused on action research:

- Use orienting statements to define the information, target, problem, or specific task to be worked on. They provide opportunity for everyone to be clear about the present focus of group work.
- Set the agenda to clarify tasks the team will work on during the meeting. Often high-priority work is focused on first, or at least early, to ensure that it will be accomplished while the energy of group members is high.
- Use summarizing statements to help the team's work accumulate. Often a recorder prints important information on poster paper or a chalkboard so that everyone is clear about what is being accomplished.
- Make procedural statements to help teammates reflect on their discussion processes. Ask members whether they want to carry on with what they are doing now or if they want to change direction.
- Take a survey, from individual to individual, to see how each member stands on an issue or a potential decision. Take a survey to get information about what members think about a certain topic. It is not a time to debate or evaluate.
- Observe which members do not say much and attempt to bring them into the discussion. People who wish to speak but can't get into the group's flow need help to contribute.
- Encourage participation of quiet members by actively supporting them to contribute.

Tip 6: Use Sound Communication Skills

Along with sound meeting skills, a cooperative action research team's performance can be enhanced by using the following communication skills:

- Paraphrase, using one's own words, to restate what another person has said. Paraphrasing allows one to understand meanings behind another person's statement.
- Describe behaviors, stating either overt behaviors of others or telling about one's own behaviors. Behavior description helps a group become focused and specific about educational issues, preferred targets, and understandings of the current situation.
- Describe feelings, pinpointing one's emotional state about an issue and putting it into clear language for others to understand. Describing feelings helps a group become focused and specific about basic values that undergird the action research.
- Make clear statements, succinctly telling others about one's ideas, using only three or four sentences. A clear statement can be accurately paraphrased by others.

Tip 7: Reach Understandings About Group Agreements

Early on, an action research team should reach agreements about how it wants to function. To form group agreements, each member should state a practice that he or she would like to see the group adopt. The group discusses each proposal until it reaches agreement. A recorder prints agreements on poster paper and later disseminates them on regular paper to everyone. From time to time, a convener reminds the group of its agreements.

Tip 8: Strive to Make Decisions by Consensus

Group consensus is a special kind of decision making that requires a thorough discussion and a spirit of cooperation. Consensus is different from a unanimous vote because it does not mean everyone agrees. Rather, group consensus means that enough group members are in favor to carry out a decision. Those who remain in doubt understand the group's decision and help with its implementation. Three steps are key to successful group consensus:

1. All members understand the issue under consideration (assessed through paraphrases and a survey).

2. All members voice their views, and the convener and recorder prod the group to reach common ground, to negotiate, and to compromise.

3. Those who doubt the decision will try it for a prescribed period without sabotaging it (a survey is also helpful here). As the action research team grows in maturity, it uses consensus decision making naturally and routinely.

Tip 9: Take Time to Debrief the Team's Group Processes

Debriefing entails an examination of the group's interaction after a meeting. The convener and recorder ask, "Are we living up to our group agreements? Are we using meeting and communication skills? How might we improve our next meeting?" Debriefing is like a small action research project as the group collects data from itself to initiate new procedures to improve its functioning.

Tip 10: Look to See if There Is Group Follow-Through

A team's efforts are only as good as the quality of its work between meetings. Most action research teams establish a division of labor as they proceed through the steps and phases. Subgroups form to prepare data collection methods, collect data, and analyze data. Group members agree to make phone calls, do library research, collect documents, and produce computer printouts. The convener and recorder, in particular, watch to see if group members follow through on group agreements made at team meetings. If follow-through does not occur, it should be a topic of group discussion during a debriefing. Figure 7.5 illustrates how a nine-member site council sought to become an effective group.

Even though effective group dynamics are essential for cooperative action research, few texts on action research address their importance. Read *Learning to Work in Groups* (Miles 1981), *The Handbook of Organization Development in Schools and Colleges* (Schmuck and Runkel 1994), *Learning Circles* (Collay, Dunlap, Enroe, and Gagnon 1998), and *Group Processes in the Classroom* (Schmuck and Schmuck 2001) for additional tips on how to achieve effective group dynamics in classrooms and schools.

Figure 7.5   A Site Council's Effective Group Dynamics

A nine-member site council of an elementary school sought to become an effective group by taking the following actions:

1. *Establish feelings of membership, inclusion, and trust.* Early in its development, the council spent a full day team building with a facilitator. The team building entailed get-acquainted activities, discussions about personal values and member self-concepts, simulations on group work, and the formation of group agreements about how the council will run its meetings and how it will transact business between meetings.

2. *Foster shared influence and dispersed leadership.* The council rotates roles of convener, recorder, and process observer throughout its membership from meeting to meeting. It strives to obtain agenda items from every member and to see that every member is involved continually in at least one of the council's projects.

3. *Accentuate friendliness and cohesiveness.* All meetings start with 20 minutes of check-in, during which each member shares something personal with the group. At holiday time, each member draws the name of another member out of a hat and gives that person a gift valued at less than $10. Members rotate the task of bringing fruit and cookies to the meetings.

4. *Cope with social status differences.* The council agrees to monitor its participation patterns to ensure that everyone gets a chance to speak and to be heard. The group agrees to use acronyms and educational jargon sparingly and to explain educational matters in plain English. Like the teachers and administrators, classified staff members and parents serve their turns as convener, recorder, and process observer.

5. *Use sound meeting skills.* In a follow-up to the day of team building, a facilitator trains the council in effective meeting skills.

6. *Use sound communication skills.* Also in a follow-up to the day of team building, a facilitator trains the council in effective communication skills.

7. *Reach understandings about group agreements.* The council keeps a handbook in which it records its group agreements. Group agreements are made during discussions in which each member states a norm or custom that he or she would like others to practice. For example, use the STP concepts during problem solving. The council discusses each proposal until it makes the agreement.

8. *Strive to make decisions by consensus.* The council agrees that it will seek a response from every member before making a decision. If members differ, creative compromises will be brainstormed. If a minority of members cannot be completely satisfied with the decision, they are asked to go along with it for a prescribed period without sabotaging it.

9. *Take time to debrief the team's group processes.* Time is set aside at the middle of every meeting to debrief the group processes. This discussion is convened by the process observer for that session.

10. *Look to see if there is group follow-through.* After check-in, the agenda for every meeting calls for a review of where the council is on each of its projects.

❈ Be Creative

Think about your own classroom and school. Think creatively about how you might do the following.

1. Establish positive social support in your classroom or in your school.

2. Incorporate critical friendship in your classroom or in your school.

3. Use probing conversation in your classroom or in your school.

4. Take leadership teaching the ten tips for group dynamics in your classroom or in your school.

❈ Reflections

Reflect on Chapter 7 by answering the following questions:

1. In what ways could cooperative action research be useful in your school or district?

2. Create examples of cooperative action research that might be possible in your school or district.

3. Identify facilitating forces in your school or district that would help cooperative action research work effectively.

4. Pinpoint restraining forces in your school or district that would hinder the success of cooperative action research. Brainstorm ways to reduce the strength of those restraining forces.

8

Types of Cooperative Action Research

A promising technique for ensuring that data are converted into action is to organize the research operations so that the group to be served, the consumers of the data, are collaborators in the planning, measurement, analysis, and interpretation of the data.

—Ronald Lippitt (1949)

The exercise of reinventing the wheel can provide an important opportunity for staff to work through and understand project precepts. . . . Without this learning by doing it is doubtful that projects attempting to achieve teacher change would be effectively implemented.

—Paul Berman and Milbrey McLaughlin (1975)

Cooperative action research has been recognized as a democratic means to local social change for quite some time, not only by action research advocates like Lippitt, but also by reviewers of traditional educational research like Berman and McLaughlin.

Almost 60 years ago, Ron Lippitt (1949) demonstrated the power of cooperative action research by using the responsive model to change intergroup relations in communities. More than 25 years later, Paul Berman and Milbrey McLaughlin (1975) did a nationwide meta-analysis of traditional research to show that effective educational innovations depended on active cooperation of local teachers and administrators in designing, implementing, and evaluating a tailored change for their own school and district.

Cooperative action research can be carried out at different system levels of a district, from one-on-one partnerships to districtwide networks of educators and their community stakeholders. Following are (1) different ways action research can be conducted under different circumstances and (2) case studies of educators conducting cooperative action research.

ONE-ON-ONE PARTNERSHIPS

One-on-one partnerships occur frequently in individual action research when one person advises or mentors another. Examples of such collaboration were presented in Chapters 5 and 6. One-on-one partnerships also occur when two people work together on a single cooperative action research project. Figure 8.1 lists typical one-on-one partnerships.

Figure 8.1   Typical One-on-One Partnerships

1. A teacher and a teacher:
   - A kindergarten teacher and a first-grade teacher perform action research to help students move from preschool to first grade.
   - A fifth-grade teacher and a second-grade teacher do action research in a cross-age tutoring program.
   - Two senior high math teachers focus on making algebra and trigonometry interesting to their students.
   - An English teacher pairs with a social studies teacher to do research on an effective division of labor to teach students to write well.

2. A teacher and a student:
   - A fourth-grade teacher and a special-needs student use action research to help improve the student's reading skills.
   - A sixth-grade teacher and a student with an attention deficit explore classroom activities that help the student stay on task.
   - A middle school teacher and a student find alternative settings for doing homework.
   - A high school coach and an athlete find a balance between athletics and academics.

3. A counselor and a student:
   - A counselor and a foreign-born third grader use action research to help the student understand the elementary school's culture.
   - A counselor and an aggressive fourth grader learn how to curb the student's tendency to start fights.
   - A counselor pairs with a middle school student to find ways to deal with the student's feelings of isolation.
   - A counselor and a twelfth grader determine signs of sexism and racism in the school.

4. An administrator and a teacher:
   - An administrator and a second-grade teacher study alternative ways to engage senior citizens as classroom assistants.
   - An administrator and a fifth-grade teacher find alternative ways to increase students' time on task.
   - An administrator and a teacher responsible for the student council convince students to take constructive action for school improvement.
   - An administrator and a high school counselor study how to help students determine what they will do after graduation.

SMALL FACE-TO-FACE GROUPS

Most cooperative action research takes place in small work groups with three to ten members who have task interdependence and hold regular face-to-face meetings. To be effective in implementing cooperative action research, group members must communicate clearly with one another, understand the primary purposes of the research, run efficient meetings, solve problems together, make decisions about project steps that are acceptable to everyone, work constructively with conflicts, and value differences within the group. Figure 8.2 lists typical small face-to-face groups.

Figure 8.2   Typical Small Face-to-Face Groups

1. One educator (a teacher, a counselor, or an administrator) with a few students drawn from different classrooms and grade levels:
   - An upper-elementary teacher cooperates with a small group of fourth, fifth, and sixth graders to study how students of that school can effectively serve a nearby senior citizens' center.
   - An elementary counselor and a small group of student representatives learn how to reduce, mediate, and manage student conflicts on the playground, in the halls, in the lunchroom, and on the way to and from school.
   - A middle school counselor and a small group of eighth and ninth graders help seventh graders feel comfortable, included, and secure in the school.
   - A high school principal and student leaders learn about managing unsportsmanlike behaviors of students and parents at competitive sports events.

2. Collegial teams of teachers from different grade levels or diverse disciplines:
   - A fourth-, a fifth-, and a sixth-grade teacher do action research on establishing, training, and managing student steering committees in their classrooms.
   - Four middle school teachers with expertise in English, social studies, science, and math develop interdisciplinary learning projects for eighth graders.
   - Five high school teachers with primary responsibility for tenth graders implement writing across the curriculum.
   - Six elementary teachers from each grade level find new ways to report students' academic performance to parents.

3. Mixed intraschool teams of teachers, counselors, specialists, and administrators with responsibility to represent their colleagues:
   - Two special educators and two regular fourth-grade teachers research ways to include special-needs students in classroom activities.
   - An administrator, two special educators, a counselor, and two teachers find alternative methods for profiling student achievement in several curriculum areas.
   - Seven teachers, each from a different elementary school, explore ways to prepare sixth graders for middle school.
   - Eight administrators, each from a different secondary school, discover ways to improve the quality of large faculty meetings.

4. Site councils or intraschool governing teams with educators, classified staff members, and parents:
   - The site council of an elementary school does cooperative action research to establish and maintain clear and open channels of communication between itself and the school's stakeholders.
   - A middle school site council researches alternative methods of classroom management.
   - A high school site council finds ways to reduce racism and prejudice within the student body.
   - A middle school site council studies a course in communication skills for seventh graders.

5. School boards from districts with diverse ethnic groups and people from all walks of life:
   - The school board of a small rural district does research to write a policy on homework.
   - A suburban school board, with a rapidly declining budget, studies how to fund extracurricular activities.
   - An urban school board studies how to improve teachers' morale.

WHOLE-SCHOOL STAFFS

Compared to small face-to-face groups with no more than two levels of hierarchy, whole-school staffs have three or more levels of line authority with more complex staff roles. Often, because of the size of a whole staff, a school's site council serves as a surrogate of the whole and becomes a catalyst of schoolwide action research. Sometimes, as illustrated below, the whole staff cooperates in action research. When that happens, the whole staff is engaged simultaneously in cooperative action research, organization development, and school change.

Proactive Projects

Whole staffs engage in cooperative, proactive action research when they participate in schoolwide inservice workshops, school-based staff development, and organization development training to bring about changes in teamwork, staff morale, school climate, and student attitudes and learning. After the interventions, they collect data to help plan the cycle of steps in proactive action research. See Figure 8.3 for topics a school staff can focus on in proactive action research.

Responsive Projects

Whole-school staffs engage in cooperative, responsive action research when they complete needs assessments, fill out school climate questionnaires, hold probing conversations about strengths and shortcomings of the school's program, or formally observe interactions at staff meetings, in one another's classes, and at extra-curricular events. Once collected and analyzed, those data give impetus to new practices, and the cycle of steps in responsive action research unfold. See Figure 8.3 for ways a staff might launch responsive action research.

DISTRICTWIDE EDUCATOR NETWORKS AND STAKEHOLDERS

Although school boards usually link educators with community stakeholders, the superintendent and board members sometimes put together an educator-stakeholder task force to tackle a specific problem through cooperative action research. See Figure 8.4 for reasons districts would establish educator-stakeholder task forces to carry out action research.

CASE STUDIES

Cooperative action research can be carried out in various ways, as illustrated by eight cases below—four are proactive and four are responsive. They do not exhaust the possibilities.

Figure 8.3   Whole-School Staff Action Research

Proactive Action Research

Whole-school staffs might engage in proactive action research to

- Assess student learning in a curriculum domain
- Improve the social-emotional climate of the staff
- Increase clear communication with parents
- Enhance inclusion of special needs students in regular classrooms
- Improve quality of staff meetings and staff development
- Increase cooperation and social support between staff and students
- Enhance students' willingness and skill in facilitating their peers' academic performance
- Improve communication channels between the whole staff and site council
- Increase abilities of teachers and students to participate effectively in cooperative learning

Responsive Action Research

Whole-school staffs might launch responsive action research to

- Assess staff members' thoughts and feelings about their own learning needs
- Check on feelings of inclusion or alienation among staff members, students, and parents
- Diagnose teachers' perceptions and feelings about the school's administrative leadership
- Assess students' understanding and performance of academic tasks
- Check staff members' reactions to group problem solving at faculty meetings
- Diagnose students' attitudes toward different teaching methods
- Assess parents' attitudes toward the school's performing arts program
- Check teachers' reactions to how administrators are implementing district policy on teacher supervision and evaluation
- Diagnose students' views about sexism and racism in their school

Figure 8.4   Educator-Stakeholder Task Forces

During the past decade, many districts have reduced their budgets and eliminated parts of programs. Some districts have formed special educator-stakeholder committees to advise the board on how to make cuts. Other districts establish educator-stakeholder task forces to carry out action research to

- Enhance the district's capacity to use computers effectively
- Improve the district's standing in its community
- Increase senior citizens' participation in school programs
- Assess citizens' perceptions of the district's strengths and shortcomings
- Check local businesspeople's perceptions of the employability of high school graduates
- Diagnose why a majority of citizens voted against constructing a new high school

One-on-One Partnership*

Robyn Mills and Irene Oswald decide to implement cross-age tutoring at Franklin Elementary. Robyn and Irene learn about it in a university course and from conversations with teachers who use it. Robyn's fifth graders will be trained to tutor Irene's second graders in math for 20 minutes, three times a week. Robyn and Irene cooperate in proactive action research to prepare training programs for fifth and second graders.

---

*All names of educators, schools, and communities have been changed.

List Hopes and Concerns

Robyn and Irene agree on the following hopes for cross-age tutoring:

- Increase second graders' knowledge and skill in math
- Enhance fifth graders' motivation and interest in math
- Foster cross-age empathy and friendship in school
- Encourage fifth graders to take responsibility for second-graders' behavior to enhance social behavior of fifth graders

Robyn and Irene also brainstorm their concerns for what could go wrong:

- A few second graders will be unresponsive tutees.
- A few fifth graders will not consider tutoring to be fun or worthwhile.
- Some fifth graders will not give accurate math information to their tutees.
- A few parents of fifth graders will complain that cross-age tutoring keeps their youngsters from learning their own fifth-grade math.

Try a New Practice

Robyn and Irene take five days to prepare their respective students for cross-age tutoring. They pair fifth and second graders according to their interpersonal compatibility and implement initial tutoring sessions three days a week for 20 minutes a day. Robyn and Irene spend 20 minutes with their own students on Fridays and Mondays to debrief them on the progress of tutoring and ways to improve it.

Collect Data

After tutoring takes place for two weeks, Robyn and Irene separately collect data from one another's students. After they learned about focus group interviews in their university course last summer, Robyn interviews second graders as an entire class. Irene conducts whole-group interviews with fifth graders. Robyn and Irene tell students they want to determine what is going well and what needs improvement in tutoring. They ask students to sit in a large circle and speak one after the other around the circle. The students explain one good thing about tutoring and one thing that could be improved. At the end of each group interview, Robyn and Irene ask students individually to complete the following sentences:

1. My tutoring partner's name is . . .

2. Compared with other ways to learn math, working with a partner is . . .

3. For me, math is . . .

4. About math, my tutoring partner feels . . .

On the following Monday, Robyn and Irene give their own students a math test.

Check What the Data Mean

Robyn and Irene analyze group interviews and sentence completion items. On Monday, they discuss their data analyses and the math test scores. From the interviews, Robyn and Irene compose a list of what is going well and what needs improvement in tutoring. For the sentence completions, Robyn and Irene use a 5-point evaluation scale to judge how many responses are highly positive, positive, neutral, negative, and highly negative. They also score math tests for accuracy. Then they brainstorm ideas about what the data mean. They decide to bring the two classes together to discuss how to improve tutoring.

Reflect on Alternative Ways to Behave

Robyn and Irene bring their classes to a media resource center. They explain the data show most students feel positively toward tutoring, although a few wish for change. Robyn and Irene take turns stating what is going well in tutoring and what needs improvement. As they go through the two lists, they stop several times to ask student pairs to generate additional ideas.

A few days later, Robyn and Irene bring their classes together again. This time they discuss four problems that need to be solved to improve tutoring:

1. Twenty minutes is often not enough time for effective math tutoring.

2. Some second graders do not do homework assigned by their tutors.

3. Some fifth graders act too tough and are not patient.

4. Some tutoring pairs do not stay on task.

Robyn and Irene ask pairs to brainstorm ways to solve these four problems. They print lists of students' ideas on poster paper.

Fine-Tune the New Practice

Robyn and Irene tell their students that tutoring will be postponed for a week so improvements can be planned. They explain that while tutoring has been successful, it can be improved in a few ways. They each work separately with their own classes.

Robyn has fifth graders role-play tutoring relationships in pairs. She teaches students to use different forms of positive reinforcement and social support. She alternates her direct instruction with role playing and coaches fifth graders on realistic homework assignments for second graders.

Irene uses pairs of second graders as part of her instruction. She asks pairs to practice math problems together, both in class and after school, to emphasize the importance of practicing math skills over and over. She has pairs discuss how they will meet to do math homework, and urges them to spend 15 minutes a day doing math problems together outside class. Irene also coaches second graders on ways to speak up to fifth graders when they feel insecure.

Robyn and Irene combine their classes again for a meeting. They ask students to sit together in tutoring pairs. Robyn summarizes what she did with fifth graders, and Irene summarizes what she did with second graders. Then they ask tutoring pairs to brainstorm ways to stay on task to learn math. On the following day, cross-age tutoring resumes. Robyn and Irene continue cross-age tutoring for the school year; subsequent data show that their hopes are actualized. (Read *Cross-Age Relationships: An Educational Resource*, Lippitt and Lohman, 1965, as Robyn and Irene did, for ideas on how to use cross-age relationships to increase student learning.)

Small Face-to-Face Groups (One Educator With Students)*

During the four years he has been a counselor at McKinley Middle School (Grades 7–9), John Mack has been impressed with the seventh graders who come to him for help with social-emotional problems. He decides to ask eight student leaders (two eighth-grade girls, two eighth-grade boys, two ninth-grade girls, and two ninth-grade boys) to cooperate with him on action research to help McKinley's seventh graders feel included and secure.

John invites eight students to eat lunch with him in the cafeteria. He tells them about his experiences with seventh graders and his desire to do action research on the problem. Then John leads the students through team-building activities to help them become better acquainted before launching action research together. John tells students about how responsive action research works and teaches them how to conduct interviews.

Collect Data

John and the eight students conduct one-on-one interviews with 72 of the 144 seventh graders at McKinley. Each member of the action research team, including John, agrees to interview eight seventh graders randomly selected from a class list. Each interview is scheduled for 30 minutes during a school day. The interviews take place over two and one-half weeks.

Prior to interviews, John, the principal, and the eight student action researchers meet with all seventh graders in the gym. The principal talks briefly about the value of a positive school climate. John introduces the idea of a cooperative action research project and the team of eight students who will work with him. John explains the first step—the one-on-one interviews—and the importance of every seventh grader participating. He explains that participation in interviews is voluntary.

Analyze the Data

After the interviews, John and the student team agree on a strategy to analyze data. They decide to construct lists of concrete examples from answers to Questions 1, 2, and 6. (See Figure 8.5 for the questions for one-on-one interviews.) For Question 3, they tally the number of times that better, about the same, and less occur for each elementary feeder school (McKinley receives students from three elementary schools). For Question 4, they give each interviewee a number and construct lists of all interviewees' extracurricular activities. For Question 5, they give each interviewee a simple yes or no and try to discern reasons for no responses. Figure 8.6 lists the themes in the data that the action research team found.

Distribute the Data and Announce Changes

John asks seventh-grade social studies teachers if his research team can use 40 minutes of social studies class time to feed data back to students. John gets approval to visit five social studies classes on one day, giving researchers an opportunity to

---

*All names of educators, schools, and communities have been changed.

Figure 8.5   Questions for One-on-One Interviews

1. Tell me what you like most about McKinley Middle School. (Probe for concrete examples.)

2. Tell me what you do not like about McKinley Middle School. (Probe for concrete examples.)

3. Which elementary school did you attend before coming to McKinley? Do you like McKinley better, about the same, or less? Please explain your answer.

4. Outside of your regular classes, are you participating in any extracurricular activities at McKinley? If yes, which ones?

5. Do your best friends attend McKinley or another school?

6. What sorts of changes at McKinley would help you feel better about going to school here? (Probe for concrete examples.)

Figure 8.6   Themes in the Data

High points of the data reveal the following themes:

- Things liked most about McKinley are competitive afterschool sports (as spectators), teachers, school spirit at pep rallies, and food choices.
- Things liked least about McKinley are a big, impersonal school, homework, eighth and ninth graders sticking among themselves, and how hard it is to get on school athletic teams.
- Students from the smallest and most rural elementary school—much more than students from the other two elementary schools—like McKinley less than their elementary school.
- Only 10 percent of seventh graders interviewed participate in extracurricular activities at McKinley—most are boys.
- About 80 percent of interviewees have best friends at McKinley; many of the 20 percent who do not have best friends come from the smallest, most rural elementary school.
- The changes that would make seventh graders feel better about McKinley are more opportunities to get to know other students, more common activities with eighth and ninth graders, seventh-grade competitive afterschool sports, and teachers giving more reasonable amounts of homework.

speak to all 144 seventh graders. The eight students on John's team form into pairs; each pair gives data feedback to one of four social studies classes. John gives feedback to the fifth class.

At the feedback sessions, researchers summarize data from Step 2 and describe changes that will probably be tried (see Figure 8.7 for the list of changes).

During the last ten minutes of each feedback session, researchers divide seventh graders into trios to obtain reactions to their ideas for change and to brainstorm additional ideas for improving student life at McKinley.

List Hopes and Concerns

John and the action team hope to

- Increase cohesiveness of the McKinley student body
- Help seventh graders feel good about school

Figure 8.7   Changes for McKinley

- The principal leads a series of cross-grade-level miniassemblies in the library. Twenty seventh graders, 20 eighth graders, and 20 ninth graders attend each miniassembly. The topic is how to increase cohesiveness of the McKinley student body.
- The PE department launches a program of intramural sports at McKinley. Each team is composed of equal numbers of seventh, eighth, and ninth graders.
- McKinley's coaches discuss the possibility of seventh-grade competitive afterschool sports.
- John leads teachers in a problem-solving discussion about McKinley's homework policy, its current implementation, and ways to improve both.

Their concerns are that

- Seventh graders from small rural elementary schools will not fit in.
- Intramural sports might separate and alienate some students rather then help them get involved in school.

Try a New Practice

The principal launches cross-grade-level miniassemblies immediately. He holds one a week for seven weeks to address all of McKinley's students. On the eighth week, the principal leads an all-student-body assembly, during which he announces various ways cohesiveness is being increased among seventh, eighth, and ninth graders.

John works with the PE department to run indoor intramural soccer games. Each soccer team comprises three seventh graders, three eighth graders, and three ninth graders. The eight student leaders on the research team volunteer to referee games in pairs.

The soccer, basketball, and track coaches initiate meetings with their counterparts in five nearby schools to discuss the feasibility of seventh-grade competitive afterschool sports.

John convenes teachers at several faculty meetings to discuss homework. Those discussions reveal that the amount of homework differs greatly from one teacher to another. The teachers decide to keep each of their homework assignments to 20 minutes, or less, per day for seventh graders.

Check Others' Reactions

John and the student leaders continue to meet as an action research team for 50 minutes once a week. Between those meetings, they collect data as follows: after dividing the 144 seventh graders by 9, each member of the research team, including John, informally observes and interviews his or her cluster of 16 seventh graders. The observations focus on participation in miniassemblies, intramural soccer, and mingling in hallways before, during, and after school. They look for indications that seventh graders are interacting with eighth and ninth graders more, the same, or less than they were before the new actions. The informal interviews focus on seventh graders' perceptions and feelings about the new actions. When researchers discuss their observations and interviews at their meetings, they seek ways to fine-tune the new actions.

Figure 8.8   Special Survey of McKinley's Seventh Graders

Please circle one answer next to each item to show whether you strongly agree, agree, feel neutral, disagree, or strongly disagree (SA, A, N, D, SD).

The principal's miniassemblies with seventh, eighth, and ninth graders have helped me meet upper-grade students.

SA   A   N   D   SD

The indoor intramural soccer program helps seventh, eighth, and ninth graders get to know one another better.

SA   A   N   D   SD

The amount of homework I must do is more reasonable now than it was earlier in the year.

SA   A   N   D   SD

I would like to see McKinley's seventh graders compete against seventh graders from other schools in track and field this coming spring.

SA   A   N   D   SD

I think McKinley's seventh graders should compete against seventh graders from other schools in soccer next fall.

SA   A   N   D   SD

I think McKinley's seventh graders should compete against seventh graders from other schools in basketball next fall.

SA   A   N   D   SD

Other changes I would like to see at McKinley are _____

_____

Collect Data

After new actions have been carried out for 15 weeks, John and the student team construct a questionnaire to administer to all seventh graders. The questionnaire has six items, each to be answered with a Likert scale. (See Figure 8.8 for the questionnaire.)

Small Face-to-Face Groups (Collegial Teacher Teams)*

Brentwood High School's principal joins five of her teachers at a statewide conference on writing across the curriculum. Since Mary Dunlap (English) and Bruce Monson (world history) were already cooperating on their writing assignments for tenth graders, the two of them asked Terri Gates (biology), Frank Leeber (geometry), and Francoise Garcia (French and Spanish) to go to a conference with them and the principal. At the conference, the new team decides to try proactive action research with writing across the curriculum for tenth graders.

List Hopes and Concerns

The team agrees on the following hopes for writing across the curriculum:

- Help students see that good writing is important in all subjects.
- Impress upon young tenth graders the importance of writing well.
- Upgrade students' writing skills through multiple feedback channels.

---

*All names of educators, schools, and communities have been changed.

The team also discusses its concerns for what might go wrong:

- Some students might complain about too much writing.
- Teachers might assign writing as homework too much and not have students write in class enough.
- Teachers might shortchange other skills because so much attention is given to writing well.

Try a New Practice

The team decides that each member will assign writing to tenth graders one day a week. Francoise chooses Monday, Frank Tuesday, Terri Wednesday, and Bruce and Mary Thursday and Friday respectively. The team of five meets once a week to discuss its new practice.

To cope with the possibility that their concerns might come true, the team also decides the following:

- Each teacher tells students, at least once a week, about the importance of learning to write well.
- Only Mary and Bruce assign writing for homework, and they will alternate that from week to week.
- Once every three weeks, the team discusses how well students seem to be learning the curriculum each teacher offers.

Collect Data

After six weeks, the team collects data on effects of its cooperative effort. Francoise and Terri prepare a questionnaire to assess tenth graders' attitudes toward writing. Frank gives a test in geometry in which students must write answers in sentences and paragraphs. Mary and Bruce score samples of students' written work for their grammatical quality. All five ask tenth graders to write a paragraph on their feelings about each class.

Check What the Data Mean

Each teacher analyzes the data he or she has collected. Frank creates a spreadsheet with student names and scores on attitudes and tests. Mary and Bruce do a content analysis of the most common weaknesses in students' writing. Terri and Francoise do a content analysis of students' feelings toward the five classes. The team meets twice during the eighth week to discuss what the data mean.

Reflect on Alternative Ways to Behave

Frank's spreadsheet shows that girls have more positive attitudes toward writing than boys. In geometry, girls' test scores (when writing answers in prose) are higher than those of boys. The team urges Frank to have boys work in critical-friendship pairs or in helping trios to get them more involved in writing. Mary and Bruce find that quite a few students write better in English class than they do in world history and biology.

Mary, Bruce, and Terri decide to trade writing samples from their classes with one another during the next three weeks. Francoise and Terri find that students feel most negative about writing in French and Spanish. The team decides to focus writing assignments for the next six weeks on English, world history, biology, and geometry. Francoise primarily emphasizes oral skills in French and Spanish.

Fine-Tune the New Practice

The team presents a panel on the program to students and their parents. The principal convenes it, emphasizing the centrality of good writing for student success in school and in life. Each teacher presents information from the action research. They end by describing changes they will make to improve the program and by reaffirming their common commitment to good writing. The principal leads parents and students in questions and answers about the tenth-grade curriculum at Brentwood. Most participants are pleased with the effectiveness of the new writing program.

Small Face-to-Face Groups (Mixed Educator Team)*

Richard Byers (counselor) and Rebecca Stein (English) chat one day about their mutual concern for negative interpersonal relations among Firgrove High School students. Both have heard students complain about one another, their teachers, and a couple of administrators. Nancy Wong (social studies) joins Richard and Rebecca to say that she has heard quite a few anti-Asian statements from students lately. Richard tells Rebecca and Nancy about a few fist fights between Caucasian and Asian boys. Rebecca adds that Bob Leaburg (coach and physical education) told her about anti-Asian sentiments he overheard among football players. Bob Leaburg sees the other three in conversation. He confirms what Rebecca said. The four decide to talk about their shared concerns with Joann Robinson (principal).

When Joann hears the concerns of the four teachers, she tells them she shares their worries. She invites them to join her to reduce anti-Asian prejudice at Firgrove and to improve school climate. Nancy tells the group about responsive action research from a class she just took at the university. All agree to cooperate for the rest of the academic year in research to improve Firgrove's social climate and, in particular, to reduce anti-Asian prejudice. Joann announces the action research to the whole staff, inviting others to communicate their perceptions to Richard Byers, who serves as chair of the responsive action research team.

Collect Data

The research team agrees with Nancy's idea to collect data via questionnaires, interviews, and observations. Drawing information from a college course, Richard introduces a questionnaire titled Student Questionnaire on Organizational Functioning, which assesses student perceptions of conflict, communication, decision making, and responsiveness between teachers and students, among the students, and among the teachers (see Schmuck and Schmuck 2001:317–319). The team tailors the questionnaire to Firgrove by modifying its language and by adding a few

---

*All names of educators, schools, and communities have been changed.

questions about prejudices and discrimination. Joann suggests collecting data in English classes, since all Firgrove students are required to take English every semester.

Nancy and Rebecca agree to work together in Rebecca's journalism class to train students to interview samples of students and staff about instances of racism and prejudice at Firgrove.

Joann, Richard, and Bob agree to create a form for structured observations in hallways, during lunch, and at assemblies and sports events. All five team members volunteer to act as observant participants in those different behavior settings during the next few weeks.

Analyze the Data

Data from questionnaires, summarized by Richard on spreadsheets, show that students perceive high conflict within the student body. What surprises the team is the high number of students who do not think the principal or teachers care about student conflicts. In fact, almost half of the students do not believe that the principal will listen to them or that teachers really want to help students solve their problems.

Results from the journalism students' interviews highlight several intergroup tensions. One concerns open conflict between male athletes and male Asian Americans. The interviewers point out, from observations during interviews, that few male Asian Americans are on sports teams and that male Asian Americans typically are better academic students than the male athletes. A second tension shows up between socially oriented females who hang around male athletes and academically oriented females who tend to run the school's music and theater projects. Teachers' observations agree with the findings of the journalism students.

Distribute the Data and Announce Changes

The research team believes that the most important target for data feedback and change is the Firgrove faculty. Team members think that the faculty has to change its relationships with students if students are to change their relationships with one another. The team forms into a panel to feed back data at a faculty meeting. Faculty members agree that they are part of the problem and would like that to change.

Joann tells the faculty that she has the superintendent's permission and the school board's approval to cancel school on the Wednesday before Thanksgiving so faculty can go on retreat together. She describes a facility in the countryside near Firgrove where the faculty will go on Tuesday after school and have time to work together until Wednesday afternoon. The main issues for the retreat is how to turn around negative energy at Firgrove and how to show students that the faculty truly is concerned about students as human beings. Joann ends the session by telling faculty that the action research team will hire a neutral facilitator to run the retreat.

List Hopes and Concerns

The Firgrove research team hopes to

- Reduce intergroup conflicts among students
- Increase friendliness among students
- Help students realize that administrators and teachers want to reduce conflicts and increase friendliness among students

Figure 8.9   Firgrove's Problems

The facilitator defines Firgrove's problems as the following:

- The situation (S) is that male athletes and male Asian Americans are engaged in unproductive conflict; the target (T) is for male athletes and male Asian Americans to feel friendly toward one another.
- The situation (S) is that some socially oriented females and some academically oriented females are engaged in unproductive conflict. The target (T) is for both groups to feel friendly toward one another.
- The situation (S) is that many students think the administration does not care about student conflicts at Firgrove. The target (T) is for students to believe that administrators are sensitive to their concerns and are trying to reduce student conflict at Firgrove.
- The situation (S) is that many students think most teachers do not care about reducing student conflicts at Firgrove. The target (T) is for students to believe that most teachers do care about their concerns and are trying to reduce student conflicts at Firgrove.
- The situation (S) is that the Firgrove faculty has no procedure to assess students' concerns. The target (T) is for Firgrove faculty members to institutionalize procedures for both assessing and acting on student concerns.

The team is concerned that

- Bringing conflicts into the open will backfire and increase conflicts.
- The retreat will not allow enough time for effective faculty problem solving.
- Some faculty members will not participate with enthusiasm.

Try a New Practice

Joann, Richard, and Nancy summarize the team's data for the facilitator, who uses the STP paradigm (Schmuck and Runkel 1994:229–265). The idea is that a problem is a gap between an unsatisfactory current situation (S) and a more desirable goal or target (T). The problem is solved, or reduced, when a path or plan (P) is found from S to T. See Figure 8.9 for the facilitator's assessment of Firgrove's problems.

The facilitator commences the retreat with a few warm-up activities and a group exercise to demonstrate how to cooperate in problem-solving groups. Next, she leads the five problem-solving groups (each with nine faculty members and a facilitator from the action research team) through the first five steps of the problem-solving sequence:

1. Specify the problem.

2. List helping and hindering forces.

3. Specify multiple solutions.

4. Plan for action.

5. Anticipate obstacles.

By Wednesday afternoon, each small group presents its action plan to the whole faculty. After the action plans are presented, the facilitator asks each group to nominate one person to work with the action research team to coordinate the follow-through of its action plan. The new group of coordinators meets with the facilitator to discuss the next steps. Figure 8.10 outlines the action ideas.

Figure 8.10   Action Ideas at Firgrove

A few action ideas from each problem-solving group are as follows:

Group 1: Get key leaders of the male athletes and male Asian Americans to run a school carnival together to raise funds for the school's media center. Have Richard and Nancy run a constructive confrontation with a sample of male athletes and a sample of male Asian Americans.

Group 2: Get key leaders of socially oriented females and academically oriented females to do STP problem solving together on the target of a supportive social-emotional climate for everyone. Have Bob and Rebecca run a series of brief get-better-acquainted activities with female students who are members of different informal subgroups.

Group 3: Have Joann visit every team, club, or other extracurricular group during the next month to listen to student concerns. The administrative team runs an annual questionnaire survey of students on some aspect of school climate.

Group 4: Assign every teacher an "advisee group" of students to counsel and mentor for 30 minutes twice a week. All English and social studies teachers present units on racism and prejudice during the next two months.

Group 5: This group also came up with ideas for an annual survey of students and of advisee groups for every teacher. It suggests too that the outside facilitator, who led the Firgrove faculty at the retreat, should carry out STP problem solving with heterogeneous groups of male and female students on reducing racism and prejudice among students.

Check Others' Reactions

The newly formed team of ten coordinators (two from each problem-solving group) decides to track faculty reactions to the retreat. Each coordinator interviews three or four colleagues about their attitudes toward the retreat and what, if anything, they are doing differently. Rebecca and Nancy ask journalism students to do a story about the retreat and its aftermath for the school newspaper. Bob lectures on character and social responsibility in his meetings with male athletes. Richard and Joann interview a sample of Asian American students.

Collect Data

Toward the end of April, the team of ten coordinators replicates the data collection of the preceding fall. Results show a better school climate at Firgrove, but improvements should still be made. Firgrove forms a School Climate Committee to continue the project another year.

Small Face-to-Face Groups (Site Council)*

Burney Elementary School (K–7), a large elementary school with 36 certified teachers, is organized into four teams: K–1, with seven regular teachers and three special educators; Grades 2–3, with six regular teachers and three special educators; Grades 4–5, with seven regular teachers and two special educators; and Grades 6–7, with seven regular teachers and one special educator.

*All names of educators, schools, and communities have been changed.

Burney is governed by a site council with nine members—four regular teachers (one from each team), one special educator (from the K–1 team), one classified staff member (a custodian), two parents, and the principal. After three training sessions in communication and meeting skills, the site council feels it's ready to communicate with Burney's stakeholders.

List Hopes and Concerns

The site council agrees on the following hopes for itself:

- Make decisions and take actions that enhance student learning.
- Solve problems cooperatively and make decisions consensually.
- Maintain clear communication channels with stakeholders.
- Lead in making Burney a healthy environment for students and staff.
- Establish strong ties with parents and other citizens in the Burney community.

Later, the site council spends an entire meeting brainstorming what members believe could go wrong:

- Reaching consensus might be difficult.
- Losing sight of students as we become engaged with one another is a possibility.
- Maintaining effective two-way communication with stakeholders might be difficult.
- Getting a lot of parents involved in the school might be challenging.

Try a New Practice

Acting on advice from the superintendent, the principal asks each site council member to serve as a communication link between the council and Burney's stakeholders. The principal links with the assistant principal, office staff members, and district office administrators. Each regular teacher links with members of his or her teaching team. The special educator helps each teacher link with special educators on each team. The custodian links with cooks, bus drivers, and one other custodian. The two parents take on the formidable task of linking to the Burney parents. The principal pledges to help the two parents find effective ways to communicate with other parents.

The new practice at Burney is an organizational structure for communication and decision making. Burney is to be a representative democracy in which the site council—as the primary governing body—strives to maintain communication channels between itself and its stakeholders.

Collect Data

After functioning together for three months, the site council divides itself into three subgroups with three members each to collect different sorts of data. Subgroup 1 (two teachers and the special educator) collects data from students. Subgroup 2 (two teachers and the custodian) collects data from staff. Subgroup 3 (two parents and the principal) collects data from parents.

Subgroup 1 uses questionnaires to collect attitudinal data from students. It also asks every teacher to rate his or her students on academic performance scales. Subgroup 2 decides to interview a sample of staff members about its perceptions of and attitudes toward the site council. Each member of the subgroup interviews six Burney staff members. The entire sample of 18 is made up of 12 teachers (3 from each team), the assistant principal, and 5 classified staff members. Subgroup 3 mails a simple one-page questionnaire to all parents to assess their awareness of, knowledge of, and attitudes toward the site council.

Check What the Data Mean

The site council meets a month later to discuss the data. Subgroup 1 finds that Burney students are happy with school and that teachers rate 85 percent of Burney students as doing "well enough" in their academic learning and social development. Two issues emerge from the data that impress subgroup members.

1. As students move through fifth, sixth, and seventh grades, they tend to become increasingly more negative toward school.

2. Most of the lowest 15 percent of students, who teachers rate as underperforming in academic learning and social development, are boys in the fifth and sixth grades.

Subgroup 2 finds that 14 of 18 interviewees perceive the site council as too separated and set off from the rest of the staff. Seven of 14 use the term *elitist* to describe the site council. Ten of 14 refer directly to lack of communication between their representative and themselves. The lack of communication is pronounced between the site council and both the subgroups for the Grades 6 and 7 team and classified personnel. Interviewees happiest with the site council are the K–1 and Subgroups 2 and 3 teams.

Subgroup 3 receives only 20 percent of parent questionnaires. The data indicate that most of the 20 percent are aware of the site council, and their attitudes toward it vary from neutral to positive. Members of Subgroup 3 decide that a 20 percent return rate is too low and that probably most parents know very little about the site council.

Reflect on Alternative Ways to Behave

The Burney site council invites an expert on site councils from its state department of education to help it find alternative ways to build communication channels to its stakeholders. The consultant leads the nine-member council through problem solving, brainstorming, and action planning. See Figure 8.11 for the results of the site council working with the expert.

Fine-Tune the New Practice

Over the rest of the school year, the site council puts ideas from Step 5 into action. By year's end, the site council has opened communication channels between itself and its stakeholders, and many more parents are taking part in Burney activities and programs. But more needs to be done, and the project continues for another year.

Figure 8.11   Results of the Burney Site Council Working With an Expert

---

The following ideas emerged from the site council working with a site council expert:

- The seven site council members who are Burney staff members will divide up each of their stakeholder groups in a new way. Instead of using formal criteria of membership to teams or to official roles in the school, the seven members will each choose five or six colleagues with whom they have frequent contact. For example, some Burney staff members drive to and from school together, see one another on weekends, attend university extension classes together, attend the same church, or have lunch together.
- The two parents and the principal will invite parents who returned the questionnaire to a special problem-solving meeting. The goal of that meeting will be to establish parent-to-parent communication channels, such as neighborhood get-togethers, a telephone or e-mail network, and parent interest groups.
- The nine-member site council will talk about itself within a fishbowl seating arrangement at an all-staff meeting at Burney. Empty chairs will be placed within the fishbowl so that members of the audience can enter the discussion to ask questions or to contribute ideas. The agenda will be to review key issues that the Burney site council is working on.
- The Burney site council will recommend that staff considers reorganizing itself into a "matrix structure." At present, the organizational structure works vertically. The teams and classified staff are separated from one another in the current structure. The challenge will be to develop cross-team and cross-classified personnel committees that will increase horizontal communication. Such cross-staff horizontal committees might focus on problems such as why older students are more negative toward school than younger students and boys have more learning problems than girls.

Small Face-to-Face Groups (School Board)*

In the rural district of Pearton, the school board's seven members discuss their concerns about lack of homework teachers assign students. In this district of 3,200 students, the homework issue goes back to the former superintendent, who moved Pearton to a policy of no homework. Now that a new superintendent has been hired, the Pearton board decides to bring up the homework policy again. The new superintendent tells the board that a homework policy could be an appropriate topic for responsive action research, which he has learned about recently at a convention of the National Rural Education Association.

Collect Data

Board members and the superintendent arrange to collect three sets of data about homework: questionnaire data from parents, interview data from superintendents of rural districts, and document data on what research says about homework and student learning.

The questionnaire, one mailed to each Pearton family with children in school, is titled Parent Attitudes Toward Student Homework From School. After a brief introductory paragraph about homework, the questionnaire starts with the following question:

About our child's/children's homework from school, we would like the teachers to assign (*please answer one*)

---

*All names of educators, schools, and communities have been changed.

1. Much more than now

2. More than now

3. The same

4. Less than now

5. Much less than now

The respondents are asked to elaborate on their answers to the questions in order to help board members and the superintendent understand respondents' reasoning.

Each board member talks by telephone with superintendents of five rural districts about their homework policies. Each interview lasts about 15 minutes. After the interviewer introduces herself or himself as a Pearton board member and comments on the board's interest in homework policies, he or she asks, "Do you have a homework policy in your school district?" If yes: "Please describe your policy" and "Will you please send me a copy?" If no: "Please tell me whether teachers give homework." And finally the interviewer uses a few probes, such as, "Can you give me an example?" or "Please tell me more about that."

A Pearton principal volunteers to do research on the Internet about homework and student learning.

Analyze the Data

The school board gets an 80 percent return on the questionnaires. The rate is high because each board member called one-seventh of Pearton households, encouraging families to respond. The results show that 77 percent of families want more or much more homework, 19 percent want the same amount, and 4 percent want less.

Of the 35 rural superintendents interviewed, 22 discuss their homework policy (20 say they have a policy to give homework, while 2 say they have a no-homework policy). Thirteen superintendents say that their districts leave homework up to teachers, with no formal homework policy; in those districts, teachers give their students homework.

The principal's report on Internet research about homework and student learning concludes that homework can enhance student learning when it provides opportunities to practice, outside of class, assignments that are discussed and reinforced in class. Thus homework is effective when it fits integrally into the teacher's in-class lesson designs. That means homework facilitates learning when students see that it fits logically into what they do in class and when teachers use it to reinforce classroom presentations and discussion.

After several discussions about the data, board members decide to hold two community meetings to advocate a pro-homework policy.

Distribute the Data and Announce Changes

Board members make another round of phone calls to Pearton families with children in school, inviting parents to attend either or both community meetings on homework. At the meetings, the superintendent presents data from Step 2, and each board member states his or her advocacy for student homework. The board chairperson then leads the audience through a question-and-answer discussion. Finally, the board members elicit ideas from parents about the quantity of homework that is reasonable. Both meetings end with the board announcing it will decide on a homework policy for Pearton at its next regular meeting.

List Hopes and Concerns

The Pearton school board hopes to

- Enhance student learning and achievement through regular homework
- Motivate teachers to administer an effective homework procedure
- Convince parents that homework can be an important facilitator of student learning

The Pearton school board is concerned that

- Some teachers might resist assigning homework because they did not have to do that during the past few years.
- Some parents will not see the importance of homework for their children.
- Some teachers will give too much homework and frustrate their students.

Try a New Practice

The Pearton school board passes a policy specifying that teachers should assign homework to students regularly to enhance students' time on tasks integral to the teachers' lesson plans. The school board also announces its support for three inservice training workshops for teachers to work out details of a homework policy.

Check Others' Reactions

During the inservice workshops, the principal documents how teachers feel about assigning homework to students. Virtually all teachers agree to have students practice assignments outside of class to enhance student internalization of teachers' lesson plans. After considerable discussion, the principal and teachers decide that 30 minutes of homework in each subject should be assigned to all high school students on Mondays, Tuesdays, Wednesdays, and Thursdays, and that once every three weeks, homework should be assigned to high school students on the weekend. For elementary and middle school students, they decide that 20 minutes of homework in each subject should be assigned on school nights, but that the elementary and the middle school students should not be assigned homework on weekends. Later, at another community meeting, the principal presents details of the homework policy to parents.

Collect Data

The following spring, four months after the new policy is in full swing, the school board launches data collections to assess how the homework policy is working. It asks the superintendent and principal to write a questionnaire, with a tailored matrix for each teacher, to measure teachers' perceptions and attitudes of the homework policy. The matrix lists students' names vertically on the left side and academic subjects across the top. To fill out the cells in the matrix, each teacher uses a 5-point scale:

1. Very high level of performance

2. High level of performance

3. Medium level of performance

4. Low level of performance

5. Very low level of performance

In an effort to gather parents' views, each board member conducts telephone interviews with 8 parents, drawn at random, making a total of 56 parent interviews. During each 15-minute interview, parents are asked about strengths and shortcomings of the homework policy, how it might be improved, and whether they want more, less, or the same amounts of homework for their children in the future. In general, data indicate that the new homework policy is working well.

Whole-School Faculty*

To engage an entire faculty in action research is logistically challenging. Some schoolwide innovations offer excellent opportunities for whole faculties to carry out self-study and cooperative reflection. Such an ideal opportunity arises at Lakeside High School, when district office administrators announce that the school will move to a block schedule and give up the traditional seven periods of 50 minutes each. The block schedule has three periods of two hours each arranged in A and B days. The A days are Monday, Wednesday, and Friday one week and Tuesday and Thursday the next; the B days are Tuesday and Thursday one week and Monday, Wednesday, and Friday the next. The mandated change presents Lakeside faculty with an opportunity for schoolwide proactive action research.

Try a New Practice

With only 15 weeks to prepare for the block schedule, the Lakeside faculty sets aside one full day and five half days for inservice training. The principal and the department heads hire consultants from a county education unit and a nearby college of education.

The consultants divide the 20-member faculty into ten critical friendship pairs. They use probing conversations to help faculty members plan how to use two hours at a time with students. As those conversations unfold, it becomes apparent that many faculty members wish to use more cooperative learning strategies and group projects in their teaching. Thus the principals and department heads decide to focus two of the five half-days on group investigation methods.

Incorporate Hopes and Concerns

During the full day of inservice training, the principal and department heads lead faculty members in a discussion about hopes and concerns. One prominent hope is to devote time to Hunter's (1982) Instructional Theory Into Practice (ITIP) lesson design. Hunter's classic ITIP lesson design calls for seven steps: (1) create an

---

*All names of educators, schools, and communities have been changed.

anticipatory set for new learning, (2) tell students what they will be learning and why it is important for them to learn it, (3) use diverse media to provide information about the objective, (4) present concrete examples of concepts, rules, or skills to be learned, (5) check to make certain students are understanding what is being presented, (6) give tasks for practice, either in class or as homework, for individualized practice, and (7) summarize what has been presented in this lesson.

In subsequent inservice sessions, the Lakeside faculty does group problem solving on the four concerns. (See Figure 8.12 for the complete list of hopes and concerns of the Lakeside faculty.)

Collect Data

The principal and department heads collect data from teachers during inservice training and from teachers and students during the first semester of block scheduling. During inservice training, the principal and department heads collect data to track the faculty's reactions and behavioral changes in three ways. Figure 8.13 explains the three ways data are collected from teachers.

The principal and department heads meet once a week from October to December to make constructive changes in the inservice training sessions.

Figure 8.12   Hopes and Concerns of the Lakeside Faculty

Hopes

- Students will learn more about each subject and perform better on statewide achievement tests by spending concentrated times on subjects.
- Teachers will give more time to each of Hunter's ITIP seven steps, with more concentrated time to teach.
- The students will experience a greater variety of teaching methods and, in particular, will become more engaged in teaching one another during cooperative learning projects.
- There will be more opportunities to give students feedback as they practice what they are being taught.

Concerns

- We will need help in understanding how best to use two-hour periods for student learning.
- More time could be wasted in off-task activities.
- Some students won't be able to stay focused mentally on the subject for two hours.
- Disruptive students could be more of a problem in block scheduling than in the traditional 50-minute period.

Figure 8.13   Three Ways Data Are Collected From Lakeside Teachers

1. The principal and department heads ask teachers to fill out postmeeting reaction questionnaires about each inservice training. The postmeeting forms ask for helpful and unhelpful things about each session and for suggestions on how to improve future sessions.

2. The principal and department heads interview three to four colleagues once every two weeks about the transition to block scheduling.

3. The principal and department heads observe faculty members' involvement in all activities during inservice training. They note whether teachers construct concrete plans for two-hour blocks of teaching and learning.

From February to June, while block scheduling is under way, the principal and department heads form the ten pairs of faculty members into five groups of four each to get everyone to collect data about Lakeside's new schedule.

One group of four presents a questionnaire on the seven steps of Hunter's (1982) ITIP for its colleagues to complete once every three weeks. With this first data set, the initiators want to remind their colleagues of the faculty's commitment to design lessons with ITIP in mind.

The second group of four creates interview statements to ask its colleagues how block scheduling does or does not facilitate student learning.

The third group administers a questionnaire to assess students' attitudes toward block scheduling.

The fourth group prepares interview questions to measure students' reactions to the block schedule and chooses 20 students at random to interview in mid-May about how to improve it.

The fifth group observes classes, focusing on teachers' use of different activity structures and students' time on task in each activity structure. Finally, the principal and department heads give achievement tests to all students at the end of May. They compare those scores with students' achievement test scores from a year ago.

Check What the Data Mean

The Lakeside faculty retreats for three days in June to check what the five sets of data mean. Each of the four-person data collection teams presents its findings and interpretations to the faculty. The principal and department heads discuss the meanings they each derive from the data in a panel.

Reflect on Alternative Ways to Behave

During the third day of its June conference, the faculty reflects on next steps to refine block scheduling. Figure 8.14 defines the key points to refine block scheduling.

Fine-Tune the New Practice

During summer, the principal prepares a class schedule that includes blocks in English, social studies, science, foreign language, and fine arts, as well as 50-minute

Figure 8.14   Key Points to Refine Block Scheduling at Lakeside

The faculty should receive more training in the seven steps of ITIP and in alternative ways to implement cooperative learning.

- Pairs of faculty members will design more two-hour blocks together.
- Some revision will be made in the class schedule so that math and physical education classes can be 50 minutes every day, rather than two hours every other day. All other curriculum domains will continue with the block schedule.
- The faculty will spend the first day of school in September orienting students to block scheduling. The orientation will include information about the faculty's aspirations for the program, its concerns about what might go wrong, and its up-to-date group agreements about how it plans to cope with its concerns.

daily periods in math and physical education. In August, the Lakeside faculty spends one day reflecting on Step 5 and planning details of its orientation day with students. Lakeside's new block schedule is becoming institutionalized.

Educator-Stakeholder Task Force*

The superintendent and school board members wish to take stock of how Hamilton's citizens view their schools. They appoint a 15-member educator-stakeholder task force to execute the study. The superintendent asks the high school principal to chair the task force. To form it, the superintendent and principal nominate seven teachers, and the seven board members each nominate one Hamilton citizen. The superintendent and board members ask the task force to gather information to assess citizens' views about the district's strengths and shortcomings and to advise on policies to improve the schools' effectiveness in the community. The high school principal and one of the task force's teachers tell the task force about cooperative, responsive action research. They use the term *needs assessment* to commence the research, defining *needs* as current conditions in Hamilton schools that should be improved.

Collect Data

The task force decides to use formal telephone interviews to collect data. Two teachers draw a random sample of 150 Hamilton citizens. Each task force member agrees to interview ten citizens. Figure 8.15 lists the three open-ended interview questions.

For more data, the task force uses content from interviews to prepare a structured questionnaire. The questionnaire has four sections:

1. A list of ten strengths, each accompanied by a Likert scale

2. A list of eight shortcomings, each with a Likert scale

3. A list of eight conditions that should be improved, each accompanied by a 3-point scale

4. A list of demographic questions, including queries about age, sex, and number of children in school

For ease of analysis, the questionnaire is printed so that the answers can be mechanically scanned. It is mailed to every household in Hamilton.

Analyze the Data

Results reveal that Hamilton's citizens agree on the schools' strengths, but they agree less on its shortcomings. Of the shortcomings that call for improvement, the four that are most frequently mentioned are

1. Ensuring student safety

2. Engaging senior citizens more in school programs

---

*All names of educators, schools, and communities have been changed.

Figure 8.15   Three Open-Ended Interview Questions

1. What do you see as strengths of Hamilton's schools?

2. What do you see as shortcomings of Hamilton's schools?

3. What conditions would you like to see improved in Hamilton's schools?

3. Upgrading facilities for handicapped access

4. Modernizing computer systems in schools

The task force finds that 78 percent of the returned questionnaires were filled out by mothers with children in school. Many citizens without children in school did not return the questionnaire.

Distribute the Data and Announce Hopes

The task force holds community meetings to feed back the data and collect more reactions from attendees. Since only 35 citizens attended the first meeting at the high school, task force members decide to hold subsequent meetings in homes. They divide into pairs (one educator and one stakeholder in each pair) to run seven meetings throughout various neighborhoods in Hamilton. Discussions in people's homes bring out two more needs for change: opening the schools to community organizations and controlling student behaviors at evening sports events. The task force announces that it hopes to respond effectively to community concerns and that it will make policy recommendations to the school board in a month.

Try a New Practice

The task force makes four recommendations to the school board. Figure 8.16 outlines the task force's recommendations.

The school board acts on Recommendations 1 and 4 by posting a bond issue and by establishing a policy that once every two years, Hamilton citizens will be surveyed for their perceptions of needs for school improvement. The school board also asks the superintendent to organize strategies to work on Recommendations 2 and 3. In turn, the superintendent engages the administrative cabinet (principals, curriculum director, and business manager) in its own action research about the community school concept. The administrative cabinet appoints a five-person committee of high school teachers to meet with police about student safety and student behavior at evening sports events.

For the community school concept, the middle school staff agrees to try a model from Flint, Michigan, for a few years. (The Flint schools remain open through the evening hours to sponsor educational and social programs for adults residing in the neighborhood of the school.) In relation to student safety, high school faculty members agree to address student safety as a problem-solving topic in social studies classes and to participate more actively with students at evening sports events.

Figure 8.16   Task Force Recommendations

The task force makes four recommendations to the school board:

1. Initiate a bond issue to modernize facilities for handicapped access and the schools' computer systems.
2. Experiment with a community school program so that more citizens without children in school can participate in school-sponsored programs.
3. Collaborate with Hamilton's police to enhance student safety and to control unruly student behavior at evening sports events.
4. Make this community assessment of needs for school improvement a regular and routine part of the district's program.

Check Others' Reactions

Each board member makes 10 to 15 phone calls to check citizens' reactions to the bond issue. With those data, the school board makes a few changes in the wording of the bond issue, offers it to the public for a vote, and wins the support of 54 percent of voters.

The administrative cabinet studies citizens' participation in the community school program and determines whether citizens without children in school increase their participation.

The high school principal, along with department heads, collects data on complaints of students, teachers, and parents about safety and behavior at sports events.

Collect Data

The school board holds a public meeting at the end of the school year to elicit citizens' reactions to (1) the community school program at the middle school, (2) student safety in the schools, and (3) student behavior at evening sports events. At that meeting, board members listen to citizens' statements, record points that most participants agree on, and ask all participants to complete a postmeeting reaction form on effectiveness of meeting procedures. At its next meeting, the school board announces that once every two years it will sponsor a survey of citizens' perceptions of the school districts' strengths, shortcomings, and needs for improvement.

Reflections

Reflect on Chapter 8 by creatively answering the following items:

1. For your school, create a plausible scenario for action research with
   - A one-on-one partnership, one educator with students, a collegial teacher team, a mixed educator team, the site council, or the whole faculty

2. For your district, create a plausible scenario for action research with
   - The school board or an educator-stakeholder task force

3. Pick two that you think are realistic possibilities. Explain.

9

Prominent Authors on Action Research

This goal of teachers to be professional problem solvers who are committed to improving both their own practice and student outcomes provides a powerful reason to practice action research.

—Geoffrey Mills (2003)

As long as we are purposely engaged in the action research process and see evidence that we are continuing to learn our way forward along the road to universal student success, we can anticipate a career of celebrations.

—Richard Sagor (2005)

Listen! The twenty-first-century voices of Mills (2003) and Sagor (2005) proclaim the value of what is known today as teacher research. Both contemporary authors expand our understanding of how much, in a century, educational action research has matured. Rooted in democratic philosophy of the first half of the twentieth century, it developed into a viable scientific alternative to traditional research during the twentieth century's second half.

ITS DEMOCRATIC PHILOSOPHICAL ROOTS

The ends of educational action research are improved professional practice and enhanced student learning; the means are democratic group dynamics. Growth and vitality of action research in twenty-first-century schools prove that research methods can become properties of everyone. Students, teachers, and administrators together can implement systematic data collection, critical data analysis, and problem solving about better actions to take.

Action research can foster individual freedom by increasing everyone's opportunity to search and choose alternative actions. Each participant's input is relevant; everyone has a voice in shaping new actions and better outcomes. The ultimate event of cooperative action research is synergy, when the quality of products of collective thought are better than the sum of the products of each individual working solo. With synergy, every participant's freedom of choice is enhanced.

Action research fosters social equality when participants value partnerships, cross-role cooperation, and cross-generational teams. Each participant's contribution is significant, regardless of age, ethnicity, sex, race, or social position. Another ultimate effect of cooperative action research is community, when all feel included, productive, and valued. As action research results in community, everyone's well-being is enhanced.

Through collection of their own data, teachers listen to voices of their students. By collecting data from teachers, administrators open their minds to input from them. By cooperating with one another, students, teachers, and administrators show appreciation and respect for the contributions of one another. Action research without democratic group dynamics will not be effective.

JOHN DEWEY, MARY PARKER FOLLETT, AND KURT LEWIN

After Dewey, Follett, and Lewin presented their conceptual hopes and democratic values, a number of applied social psychologists and change-oriented educators contributed prominently to a rapidly expanding literature on educational action research.

John Dewey

A high school and university teacher, John Dewey became America's best-known and most prolific educational philosopher. He considered democracy to be a quality of living together—a mode of community life—rather than just a form of government.

At the turn of the twentieth century, when members of diverse ethnic groups were coming together in neighborhoods of Chicago and New York, Dewey conceptualized how to foster their cohesion and togetherness. He viewed public schooling as a primary means for achieving social integration. He argued that schooling should embody democracy in action, thereby serving as a microcosm and mirror of the larger democratic community.

Through democratic participation in classrooms, Dewey believed that students would learn concepts, values, and skills of cooperative living. He thought that group projects, in which students cooperate to reflect on and study social issues or community problems, would offer an important means for achieving a more democratic community.

Dewey's ideas about group projects resembled teacher-student and student-student cooperative action research. He argued too that teachers and administrators should work together democratically, not only because it is a moral way to run a school, but also because students could observe adults modeling democratic norms and procedures.

Mary Parker Follett

Author of four books and a popular lecturer on workplace democracy, Mary Parker Follett sought to use scientific methods to transform worker-manager conflict into creative solutions to enhance productivity. Like Dewey, she considered democracy as daily social interaction rather than as only a form of government. She believed that conflict in industrial organizations is natural and inevitable, arguing that intergroup conflict can be harnessed to increase organizational effectiveness. She told audiences, "All polishing is done by friction" (Follett 1940:31). She taught workers and managers to bring their differences to joint conferences and to use scientific methods in resolving conflicts together.

Follett (1965) conceptualized four critical steps for workers and managers to achieve a harmonious relationship. Her key concept was "coordination." First is coordination by virtue of frequent face-to-face meetings of responsible parties. Second is coordination of participants to specify and define problems they have in common. Third is coordination of participants studying all aspects of problems together. Fourth is coordination of continual intergroup problem solving.

Kurt Lewin

Kurt Lewin is the grandfather of action research. He was born on the ninth day of the ninth month in the 90th year of the nineteenth century. Lewin emigrated from Germany in 1933 because, as a Jew, he could not qualify for a tenured professorship at the University of Berlin. The discrimination and prejudice he observed throughout his time in Central Europe, along with the frightening rise of Nazism, motivated him to look for ways that social science could help strengthen democracy and reduce prejudice. Lewin thought of action research and democratic participation as synonymous.

During his 14 years in the United States, he collaborated with dozens of outstanding students and coworkers at Cornell, Iowa, and the Massachusetts Institute of Technology. Although he sought to integrate traditional science with action research, his collaborators spent most of their time and effort publishing traditional research, because promotion to full professor required publication of traditional research in scholarly journals.

Lewin too published his research primarily in scholarly journals. A notable exception was *Resolving Social Conflicts* (1948), edited by his wife, Gertrud Weiss Lewin, one year after his death. That collection of Lewin's work includes examples of his community-based action research during World War II. In the Foreword, Gordon Allport wrote: "There is a striking kinship between Kurt Lewin and John Dewey. Both agree (although they never met each other) that democracy must be learned anew in each generation and that it is a far more difficult form of social structure to attain and maintain than is autocracy."

Lewin was dedicated and hard working; he had time for every student and colleague and was enormously influential in meetings. Many of his students and coworkers undoubtedly carried out a good deal of unpublished action research as consultants and social activists. Lewin truly believed in the value of human interdependence and sought to build bridges between practitioners and scientists.

Lewin's contributions to action research are alive today. In September 2004, on his 114th birthday, Polish and German social psychologists, led by Janusz Trempa, organized an International Conference on Kurt Lewin's Contributions to Contemporary Psychology, sponsored by the University of Bydgoszcz (pronounced Be-go-sh). Bydgoszcz, Poland, is close to Mogilno, a rural town where Kurt was born and lived for his first 14 years. Along with learning how to pronounce Bydgoszcz, I learned that Kurt's surname was pronounced Lev-in in Mogilno, Le-vene in Berlin, and Lou-win in Iowa City, where his daughter, Miriam, attended elementary school. We opened a Kurt Lewin Museum in his boyhood house and created the Kurt Lewin Center at Bydgoszcz, which, among other things, runs summer workshops to prepare social scientists and educators to do action research. I am a member of the center's scientific board; sections of this book make up part of the curriculum for the center's workshops. For details, read Sherman, Schmuck, and Schmuck (2005).

ALICE MIEL AND STEPHEN COREY

Alice Miel and Stephen Corey, two pioneers in linking action research to school improvement, both worked at the Horace-Mann-Lincoln Institute of School Experimentation at Columbia University, New York. Miel applied action research to classroom improvement, while Corey focused more on cooperative action research in schools and districts.

Alice Miel

From 1944 to 1950, Alice Miel cooperated with Ken Benne (who worked with Lewin), Chandas Reid, and Alice Stewart in the Horace-Mann-Lincoln Institute of School Experimentation at Columbia University in New York. They used action research methods to help elementary school teachers use cooperative learning procedures in their classrooms. Miel and her associates consulted with over 100 teachers nationwide in one of the largest efforts ever to disseminate action research methods.

The project's teachers planned cooperative learning activities in small collegial groups for their students. They tried particular cooperative procedures in their own classes, collected systematic data about processes and effects, modified the cooperative procedures when needed, and collected additional data to track results. Miel and her associates taught teachers to collect data in several ways from several sources. The teachers amassed introspective data by keeping reflective journals about their teaching. They also collected perceptual and attitudinal data from their students, and their colleagues collected data on classroom behaviors of students during cooperative learning. The teachers also collected data from parents about their reactions to cooperative learning activities.

Miel and her associates helped teachers reflect on the data, arranged for small groups of teachers to discuss the data, and facilitated group problem solving about ways to improve cooperative learning activities. As the project unfolded, Miel and her associates taught teachers how to find scientific evidence for student growth in helpfulness, friendliness, independence, responsibility, and group skills. They also helped teachers collect data on students' cognitive growth and academic achievement in different curriculum domains. The project helped establish action research and cooperative learning as core parts of curriculum for graduate students at the Teachers College at Columbia (Miel et al. 1952).

Stephen Corey

Partly because of Miel's innovative efforts, Stephen (called "Max" by friends) Corey, then executive director of the Horace-Mann-Lincoln Institute of School Experimentation, organized three national conferences on action research to improve school practices. At one of those meetings, school administrators from Denver, Colorado, showed special interest in action research and subsequently cooperated with Corey and his staff to conceptualize action research for school administrators.

The Denver group distinguished between empirical action research and the more typical casual inquiry, which group members thought most school administrators do every day. Using empirical action research, data are systematically sought, recorded, and interpreted to discover any problems (as in responsive action research) and to learn the effect of using new procedures to solve existing problems (as in proactive action research).

The Denver group wanted to answer whether a particular action truly did result in desirable consequences. Group members labeled their question the action hypothesis. An action hypothesis of interest to high school principals in Denver was that high school curriculum committees comprising volunteers will be more productive than curriculum committees comprising appointees. The group also wished to collect data on undesirable outcomes that might accompany the expected results. The principals deliberately searched for dysfunctional outcomes, such as colleagues feeling alienated from an elite group of volunteers. Corey's administrators, like Miel's teachers, sought multiple-method data from multiple sources.

After eight years of cooperative action research projects throughout the United States, Corey (1953) came up with six conditions that foster effective school-based action research. His conditions are as true today as they were a half-century ago. See Figure 9.1 for Corey's six conditions.

RON LIPPITT

Ron Lippitt, Lewin's student who did the most to nurture the development of action research, began working with Lewin in 1936. Although Lippitt was just 24 when he joined Lewin in Iowa City, he had already spent a year studying with Jean Piaget in Geneva, Switzerland. Lewin, Lippitt, and White finished the famous democratic, autocratic, laissez-faire leadership study of boys' clubs in 1939. During World War II, Lewin and Lippitt's research focused on military needs and practical problems of soldiers.

During the 1950s, Lippitt taught planned change in the Research Center on Group Dynamics at the University of Michigan. In 1958, with students Jeanne Eisenstadt Watson and Bruce Westley, Lippitt wrote *The Dynamics of Planned Change* (1958).

Figure 9.1   Corey's Six Conditions That Foster Effective School Action Research

1. *Openness to Weakness:* Administrators and staff members speak honestly to one another about those parts of the school program that need improvement.

2. *Chances for Creativity:* Administrators provide staff members with opportunities to brainstorm and analyze inventive ideas about alternative future practices.

3. *Support for Trial and Error:* Administrators provide staff members with support, resources, and materials to initiate and test alternative practices.

4. *Cooperative Staff Relations:* Administrators and staff members share norms and skills that support cooperative problem solving about their own group efforts.

5. *Value Data Collection:* Administrators and staff members believe they should go beyond casual inquiry to collect systematic data about their processes and school outcomes.

6. *Time for Improvement:* Administrators create ways to release staff members from regular duties to become engaged in professional reflection, action research, and staff problem solving.

As a graduate student, I took Lippitt's course on planned change in 1959. I was among the first to read the new book. I collaborated and cooperated with Lippitt as a doctoral student in social psychology and as a postdoctoral fellow from 1959 to 1965. He was my most important mentor in action research. If Lewin is the grandfather of action research and Lippitt the father, then I like to count myself as a son of action research.

Although the term *action research* rarely appears in *The Dynamics of Planned Change,* the book underscores essential steps of responsive action research. Lippitt and his coauthors describe seven phases of planned change, presented in Figure 9.2.

PAULO FREIRE

Paulo Freire, an educational reformer, developed a radically innovative strategy of adult learning and social change during the 1960s in Brazil and Chile. Freire (1970) likened traditional education to a bank where teachers deposit knowledge into students, who serve as depositories. The proper role of a student is to receive, to file, to store, and, when called upon, to issue the deposits.

While teaching illiterate adults to read and to feel empowered to change their impoverished lives, Freire thought of teaching and learning as a mutually interactive exchange—learners teach and learn at the same time. Adult development occurs in groups. The group process of learning together focuses on creative problem solving, during which participants reflect on their situations. At the same time, participants are learning to read. The psychological keys to learning to read are reflection about oneself, discussion about others' reflections, and cooperation with peers to change things for the better. Reading, reflecting, feeling empowered, and cooperating to solve problems cannot be separated.

Just as professional reflection is linked to action research, self-reflection is linked to improving one's own situation. Although Freire writes very little about systematic data collections in his pedagogical strategy, his stress on interpersonal dialogue assumes that it is through open and honest exchanges of personal information—or as we have called it, "probing conversation"—that adult learners grow. People grow

Figure 9.2   Seven Phases of Planned Change

Phase 1: An individual or team pinpoints a need for change. Although the need for change might emanate from frustration, the individual or team strives to define the need as a current situation falling short of a target or ideal state.

Phase 2: Systematic data are collected about the current situation and the participants' wishes for the ideal state. The data come from multiple sources.

Phase 3: The data are used to create a diagnosis of the situation. This phase can include the force field analysis (see Chapter 1), which Lewin conceptualized as part of his field theory.

Phase 4: After the diagnosis, a plan is made to change the current situation and move toward the ideal state. This phase is the heart of planned change; it must be guided by data for it to be action research.

Phase 5: The plans of Phase 4 are converted into actual change efforts—these efforts are the actions of action research.

Phase 6: The actions are assessed. (Are the change efforts working?) Systematic data are collected.

Phase 7: The best parts of the actions are institutionalized.

---

intellectually and emotionally when they grapple with thoughts, feelings, and skills of others. In that sense, Freire views dialogue as exchanges of data to help participants improve their own lives.

REGINALD REVANS

Another unique reformer was Reginald Revans of Great Britain, who developed an organizational improvement strategy called action learning. During World War II, Revans noted that people who helped neighbors in trouble were themselves subsequently better able to cope with similar challenges.

During the 1950s and 1960s, Revans used that insight to create the consultative strategy of action learning in coal mines, hospitals, and local governments. In action learning, organizations with the same functions, such as two mines, two hospitals, or two local governments, pair off to help each other improve.

Applied to education, a team of administrators, teachers, and students of one school pairs off with a similar team of a neighboring school. The consultative role of each team is, in relation to its neighbor, to collect diagnostic data, feed back the data analysis, and lead it through problem solving to create change. Through mutual exchanges of help, not only does the receiving team learn about what to change in its school, but so does the giving team learn about ways to change its own school.

To translate Revans's action learning into the focus of this book, we could say that by helping carry out action research in neighboring classrooms or schools, you learn better how to do effective action research in your own classroom or school. Read Revans (1982) to learn about action learning.

CHRIS ARGYRIS AND DONALD SCHÖN

Chris Argyris and Donald Schön are action scientists, a variation of action researchers. Action scientists study what social-psychological dynamics are present in a concrete social situation. They review published research that might shed light on that particular situation, plan strategies to change the status quo, intervene to improve the situation, evaluate how improvements unfold and interrelate, plan revised strategies and interventions, and then continually plan, intervene, and evaluate. As these cycles of action and research play out, action scientists strive to create general principles and hypotheses that serve as building blocks of scientific theories of planned social change.

Chris Argyris

Chris Argyris created action science with Harvard University students during the 1970s and early 1980s. In action science, a bundle of interrelated intellectual and behavioral events produce (1) concrete data for local action, problem solving, and improvement and (2) general principles for scientific theories of planned change. Like Lewin, Argyris hoped to build bridges between practical action researchers and theoretical social scientists (Argyris, Putnam, and Smith 1985).

Many traditional social scientists believe that their knowledge contributes to the work of action researchers; however, they often do not believe that knowledge gleaned from local action research contributes to development of more general theory. Argyris, like Lewin, does not agree. Argyris argues that traditional social scientists can learn a great deal by studying how action researchers go about changing things. He offers Lewin's force field analysis as a case in point.

Donald Schön

Donald Schön (1983 and 1987), Argyris's colleague at Harvard, contributed to our understanding of how professional reflection can facilitate improved practice. Schön sees reflective practice engaging teachers, administrators, or students in cycles of introspection and action, based on their experiences in the classroom and in school. During reflection, according to Schön, mature professionals think critically about their plans, decisions, actions, and effects on others to improve them tomorrow, next week, or next month. As educators introspect about their past and present actions, they create concepts, hopes, and concerns to guide their future actions.

Schön writes about reflection on action and reflection in action. Reflection on action entails thinking critically about one's actions after they have had an effect (e.g., reflecting on one's achievements and failures with a particular lesson plan). Reflection in action entails thinking critically about one's actions in the midst of action (e.g., reflecting on others' reactions to a lesson being taught). Schön's two types of reflection offer data, in the style of a personal action research project, to plan for future changes. The art of personal and group reflection about past, present, and future events are integral processes of action research.

STEPHEN KEMMIS AND JEAN MCNIFF

Stephen Kemmis and Jean McNiff, prominent proponents of action research in the 1980s, did most of their work in England. More recently, Kemmis has been facilitating school-based action research in Australia.

Figure 9.3   Self-Reflective Cycle

A teacher realizes she is unhappy with student involvement in social studies (planning). Although she cannot change the prescribed curriculum, she can change how students work within the curriculum. She decides to use helping trios in social studies instruction. The teacher explains to students how helping trios work, and she forms students into trios (acting). Next, she listens in on a few trios to assess how they are going (observing). She is pleased with student energy and involvement, but she is worried about too little student time on task (reflecting). The teacher decides to train students in how to use a structured interview within trios (planning). She carries out the training (acting). Then she listens in on a few trios (observing). She likes what is happening in general (observing); however, she is concerned about four of her special-needs students who are not as highly involved as the other students. Thus self-reflective cycles of personal action research continue.

Stephen Kemmis

Taking cues from Schön, Stephen Kemmis's primary concern is in helping teachers critically reflect on their practice. He is more concerned with teacher intro-spection and teacher-teacher dialogue about practice than he is with the collection of systematic data using questionnaires, interviews, or documents. Kemmis's main research method is teachers making critical observations of their own practice (Kemmis and McTaggart 1988).

In *The Action Research Planner*, Kemmis and McTaggart (1988) delineate their self-reflective cycle—plan, act, observe, reflect, and plan, act, observe, reflect, and so on. For an example of the self-reflective cycle, see Figure 9.3.

Jean McNiff

Jean McNiff has extended Corey's, Lippitt's, and Kemmis's work in educational action research. In her book *Action Research: Principles and Practice*, McNiff (1997) describes the conceptual and historical bases of action research. She outlines how to start an action research project and describes various data collection techniques that are readily available to teachers.

McNiff urges educators to start small when they initiate their first action research project. Teachers or administrators should start with their own personal, small-scale projects, or teachers and administrators should start with cooperative action research that is narrowly focused. McNiff stresses careful and deliberate planning, a realistic timetable for data collection, careful involvement of key stakeholders, and the establishment of clear and open communication with relevant administrators. Her book is replete with case studies of action research and includes tips on how to establish a collaborative network of action researchers.

WILLIAM FOOTE WHYTE

In 1991, William Foote Whyte edited *Participatory Action Research*, which presents case studies of action research in industry and agriculture. Whyte's text does not give information about educational action research. Names like Dewey, Follett, Lewin, Miel, Corey, Lippitt, and Freire are notably absent from it, but Whyte's book adds to our understanding of the multiple roots of action research.

Figure 9.4   Whyte's Intellectual Streams

---

1. *The participatory research methods of social anthropologists and sociologists.* Participatory research methods, such as participant observation, have not been popular in psychology, where questionnaires, interviews, and documents often prevail. Whyte emphasizes observations made by participants themselves (e.g., group members serving as process observers, individual participants keeping journals about their own experiences, and nonparticipants watching action research participants throughout different phases of action research).

2. *The participation of lower-echelon workers in organizational decision making.* Whyte refers to innovations aimed at democratizing the workplace, such as organizational development, total quality management, and quality of work-life programs. He argues that once workers participate with management in decision making, the idea of active cooperation between management and labor in a research process becomes legitimate. In that sense, Whyte views the rise of action research as depending on previous acceptance of worker participation in administrative matters.

3. *The concept that worker behavior depends on a combination of cultural and technological variables.* Whyte refers to the one-sided nature of Frederick Taylor's technocratic strategy of scientific management. Whyte argues that as scientific managers were influenced by the human relations movement to seek an integration between the human side and the technical side of the workplace, they could also recognize the benefit of engaging workers in action research to improve productivity. Thus what has come to be called sociotechnical theory lends intellectual support to the idea of participatory action research.

Whyte argues that action research in industry and agriculture flows out of three intellectual streams in social science. Figure 9.4 explains these three intellectual streams.

RICHARD SAGOR

Richard Sagor's *How to Conduct Collaborative Action Research,* published in 1992 by the Association for Supervision and Curriculum Development (ASCD), is a small but impressive text. It presents background information on why educators need cooperative action research, what it is, and how to put it into a school or district.

Sagor offers five sequential steps, which are similar to the first four steps of responsive action research. Figure 9.5 highlights the five steps.

Another helpful aspect of Sagor's book is the practical information he gives about the three data sets mentioned in Step 2.

In a more comprehensive book, *The Action Research Guidebook,* compared to his earlier contributions, Sagor (2005) guides you step by step through action research. He subtitles the book *A Four-Step Process for Educators and School Teams.* The steps or stages are as follows:

- Clarifying vision and targets, where you ask: What do I want to accomplish?
- Articulating theory, where you ask: What do I believe is the approach with the greatest potential for achieving my goals?
- Implementing action and collecting data, where you ask: What data will I need to collect to understand the efficacy and workings of my theory of action?
- Reflecting on the data and planning informed action, where you ask: Based on the data, how should I adjust my future teaching?

Figure 9.5 Sagor's Five Sequential Steps

Step 1: A problem of great concern is defined and analyzed. Borrowing from the creative work of Peter Holly and Gene Southworth (1989), Sagor describes how to use graphic flowcharts to depict interconnected parts of an educational problem.

Step 2: Data are collected about the problem. Sagor argues that at least three data sets (existing data, methods to assess everyday life, and questioning methods) should be gathered for each problem. The first data set concerns records that already exist, such as student files, attendance data, teacher records about student behavior, and portfolios of student work. The second set, methods to assess everyday life, includes student and teacher journals, audio or video recordings of classroom activities, visitors' perceptions and reactions, systematic observations (both structured and unstructured), and photographs of classroom activity structures and of students in various school settings outside the classroom. The third set, questioning methods, includes individual and focus group interviews, paper-and-pencil questionnaires (including sociometric inventories), and achievement tests.

Step 3: The data are analyzed for themes and patterns. Sagor presents the idea of a data matrix as a useful device for organizing data and pinpointing themes.

Step 4: The results of the data analysis are reported to significant stakeholders. Sagor gives helpful ideas on how to structure the report.

Step 5: A plan for action is prepared and implemented. Sagor advocates using Lewin's force field analysis to develop action plans.

GEOFFREY MILLS

Geoff Mills's guide (2003) for the teacher researcher is on my list of ten essential books to read to extend and deepen your information about educational action research. In this helpful user-friendly text, Mills offers a thorough analysis of action research for teachers. He helps you understand action research, decide on a focus for it, select data collection techniques, analyze and interpret the data, and plan actions for educational change. In particular, Mills zeroes in on qualitative data collection procedures; he offers rich discussions on taking field notes and doing informal, ethnographic interviews. He also presents guidelines and tips for writing up your action research for publication and dissemination.

After you finish reading this last chapter of my book, consider reading my selections for the educator's essential action research library listed in Figure 9.6.

TEACHER RESEARCH

The historical movement from Lewin, Corey, Lippitt, and Barnes to Kemmis, McNiff, Hollingsworth, Mills, and Sagor is in the upward direction of making action research more accessible to busy, overloaded, and underappreciated teachers and administrators. The most recent prominent authors write about practical, down-to-earth research methods that can readily be applied to real classrooms in real schools. They seek too to establish educator networks so that colleagues can support one another in doing teacher research.

Teacher research is classroom or school-based action research, carried out by teachers, published by teachers, and disseminated from teacher to teacher for the enrichment of teachers. (I could substitute *roles*, such as administrators, counselors,

Figure 9.6   The Educator's Essential Action Research Library

1948 Lewin, K., *Resolving Social Conflicts*

1953 Corey, S. M., *Action Research to Improve School Practices*

1958 Lippitt, R., J. E. Watson, and B. Westley, *The Dynamics of Planned Change*

1960 Barnes, J. B., *Educational Research for Classroom Teachers*

1983 Schön, D., *The Reflective Practitioner*

1988 Kemmis, S., and R. McTaggart, *The Action Research Planner*

1997 McNiff, J., *Action Research: Principles and Practice*

1997 Hollingsworth, S. (ed.), *International Action Research*

2003 Mills, G. E., *Action Research: A Guide for the Teacher Researcher*

2005 Sagor, R., *The Action Research Guidebook*

specialists, boards, and the like, for teachers, but to close this book I wish to empha-size *teachers*.)

Teacher research has grown in Australia, Canada, England, Central Europe, Scandinavia, and the United States. Stephen Kemmis and Robert McTaggart wrote about teacher research in Australia in the 1980s and have developed waves of teacher researchers. One of them, Catherine Kebir, took her action research on adult learners to the 1992 Convention of Teachers of English to Speakers of Other Languages (TESOL) in Vancouver, B.C., Canada, and found many Canadian teach-ers ready to do action research. Since that time, I have taught action research to over 200 receptive Western Canadian teachers, and my friend, Michael Fullan, the inter-nationally known Canadian scholar, has been a strong advocate of teacher research in Ontario. Jean McNiff, Peter Holly, and Robert Stenhouse are prominent English advocates of teacher research, while Jan Trempa, director of the Kurt Lewin Center at the University of Bydgoszcz, Poland, runs summer workshops on action research for young educators. Per Dalin, Per Kvist, Ivar Njerve, and Svend Skyom Nielsen have been strong proponents and teachers of teacher research in Norway, Sweden, and Denmark for over 25 years. Emily Calhoun, Cathy Caro-Bruce, Sandra Hollingsworth, Ruth Hubbard, Geoff Mills, Brenda Power, and Richard Sagor in the United States have led in writing about this new discipline of teacher research, cre-ating a living body of classroom research that resonates with John Dewey's quintes-sential American vision of a more democratic and useful social science.

The new discipline of teacher research is being fueled by three reform move-ments in the educational systems of third world countries. First is the constructivist, in contrast to the positivist, position that teachers can create a useful knowledge base about teaching and learning. In reality, teachers build theory and do informal research every day; we should codify and legitimize those efforts. Second is critical theory, in contrast to the elitist, position that teachers, who have been powerless and silent toward traditional educational research, have an important contribution to make in producing knowledge about teaching and learning. Third is the feminist, in contrast to male-dominated, position that elementary teachers (mostly women) and children (the young students) can contribute to a more comprehensive and humane theory to explain how teaching and learning really operate in classrooms.

I estimate the teacher research movement to be in its second decade of development. You can still read all issues of the professional journal *Educational Action Research*. The contributions, mostly case studies by teachers about their own classrooms, report on action research projects as well as special instances of self-reflection and critical self-analysis to solve student problems. Read the 50 or so master's theses, or as they are called, the Individual Research Projects (IRP), of the LEE Fellows (Leadership for Educational Entrepreneurs) of Arizona State University–West. Each is a practical action research project by a maturing educator. Read too the 15 articles in Schmuck (2000). Your reading will show you that the past inspirational leadership of Dewey, Follett, and Lewin are becoming present classroom and school realities.

Reflections

Reflect on Chapter 9 by answering the following questions:

1. Which three prominent authors on action research do you relate to most closely? Explain the reasons.

2. Which five ideas of the 15 prominent authors would you like to incorporate into your own professional repertoire as an action researcher?

3. How might you contribute to the teacher research movement?

Bibliography

Argyris, C., R. Putnam, and D. M. Smith. 1985. *Action Science*. San Francisco, CA: Jossey-Bass.

Aronson, E. 1978. *The Jigsaw Classroom*. Beverly Hills, CA: Sage.

Barnes, J. B. 1960. *Educational Research for Classroom Teachers*. New York: Putnam.

Beattie, A. 1986. *Where You'll Find Me and Other Stories*. New York: Macmillan.

Berman, P. and M. McLaughlin. 1975. *Federal Programs Supporting Educational Change*. Vol. 6, *The Findings in Review*. Santa Monica, CA: RAND.

Boehlert, S. R. 2004. *Increasing Parental Involvement in a Charter School*. Phoenix, AZ: ASU-West, LEE Program in College of Education.

Bradford, L., J. Gibb, and K. Benne, eds. 1964. *T-Group Theory and Laboratory Method*. New York: John Wiley & Sons.

Campbell, L. 2003. *Mindful Learning: 101 Proven Strategies for Student and Teacher Success*. Thousand Oaks, CA: Corwin Press.

Coch, L. and J. French. 1948. "Overcoming Resistance to Change." *Human Relations* 4:512–32.

Collay, M., D. Dunlap, W. Enroe, and G. Gagnon. 1998. *Learning Circles*. Thousand Oaks, CA: Corwin Press.

Corey, S. M. 1953. *Action Research to Improve School Practices*. New York: Bureau of Publications, Teachers College, Columbia University.

Darroch, B. J. 2004. *Singapore Math: Action Research on a Curriculum Change, Elementary Student Achievement, and Teacher Efficacy*. Phoenix, AZ: ASU-West, LEE Program in College of Education.

Dewey, J. 1916. *Democracy and Education*. New York: Free Press.

———. 1933. *How We Think*. Boston, MA: Heath.

———. 1939. *Intelligence in the Modern World: John Dewey's Philosophy*, edited by J. Ratner. New York: Modern Library.

Follett, M. P. 1924. *Creative Experience*. New York: Longman's.

———. 1940. *Dynamic Administration*. New York: Harper & Brothers.

———. 1965. *The New State: Group Organization, the Solution of Popular Government*. 2d ed. Gloucester, MA: Peter Smith.

Fox, R. and R. Lippitt. 1964. "The Innovation of Classroom Mental Health Practices." In *Innovation in Education*, edited by M. B. Miles. New York: Teachers College, Columbia University.

Fox, R., M. Luszki, and R. A. Schmuck. 1966. *Diagnosing Classroom Learning Environments*. Chicago, IL: Science Research Associates.

Freire, P. 1970. *Pedagogy of the Oppressed*. New York: Herder & Herder.

Grant, L. 2004. *The Business Managers' Network: Action Research to Improve Business Capacities of Colorado Charter Schools*. Phoenix, AZ: ASU-West, LEE Program in College of Education.

Hall, G. E. and S. M. Hord. 1987. *Change in Schools: Facilitating the Process*. Albany, NY: State University of New York Press.

Heidegger, M. 1962. *Being and Time*. New York: Harper.

Hess, R. T. 1996. "Writing Process, Portfolios, and Programs: Teacher Action Research." Unpublished master's thesis, Oregon State University, Corvallis, OR.

Hollingsworth, S. 1994. *Teacher Research and Urban Literacy Education: Lessons and Conversations in a Feminist Key*. New York: Teachers College Press.

———, ed. 1997. *International Action Research: A Casebook for Educational Reform*. London, England: Falmer Press.

Holly, P. and G. Southworth. 1989. *The Developing School*. London, England: Falmer Press.

Horn, C. 2004. *Improving Reading Comprehension in the Middle Grades*. Phoenix, AZ: ASU-West, LEE Program in College of Education.

Hunter, M. 1982. *Mastery Teaching*. El Segundo, CA: Instructional Dynamics.

Januzzi, P. 2004. *Action Research on Mentoring Foreign Teachers in a French Immersion Academy*. Phoenix, AZ: ASU-West, LEE Program in College of Education.

Kebir, C. 1994. "An Action Research Look at the Communication Strategies of Adult Learners." *TESOL Journal*, Autumn, 4(1):28–31.

Keech, P. S. 2004. *Effects on Teacher Morale and Collegiality of a New Formative Evaluation System*. Phoenix, AZ: ASU-West, LEE Program in College of Education.

Kemmis, S. and R. McTaggart. 1988. *The Action Research Planner*. 3d ed. Victoria, Australia: Deakin University Press.

Kohl, H. R. 1969. *The Open Classroom: A Practical Guide to a New Way of Teaching*. New York: New York Review.

Leary, W. G. and J. S. Smith, eds. 1951. *Think Before You Write*. New York: Harcourt Brace.

Lewin, K. 1948. *Resolving Social Conflicts*. New York: Harpers.

———. 1951. *Field Theory in Social Psychology*. New York: Harpers.

Lippitt, P. and J. Lohman. 1965. "Cross-Age Relationships: An Educational Resource." *Children* 12:113–17.

Lippitt, P., J. Eisman, and R. Lippitt. 1969. *Cross-Age Helping Programs: Orientation, Training, and Related Materials*. Ann Arbor, MI: University of Michigan's Center for Research on Utilization of Scientific Knowledge, Institute for Social Research.

Lippitt, R. 1949. *Training in Community Relations: Toward New Group Skills*. New York: Harper.

Lippitt, R., J. E. Watson, and B. Westley. 1958. *The Dynamics of Planned Change*. New York: Harcourt Brace.

Marrow, A. J. 1969. *The Practical Theorist: The Life and Work of Kurt Lewin*. New York: Basic.

McNiff, J. 1997. *Action Research: Principles and Practice*. London, England: Routledge.

McNiff, J. and J. Whitehead. 2000. *Action Research in Organizations*. New York: Routledge.

Mead, G. H. 1934. *Mind, Self, and Society*. Chicago, IL: University of Chicago Press.

Mendoza, A. 2004. *Administrative Mentoring for Effective Leadership*. Phoenix, AZ: ASU-West, LEE Program in College of Education.

Miel, A., et al. 1952. *Cooperative Procedures in Learning*. New York: Bureau of Publications, Teachers College Press, Columbia University.

Miles, M. B. 1981. *Learning to Work in Groups*. 2d ed. New York: Teachers College Press, Columbia University.

Mills, G. E. 2003. *Action Research: A Guide for the Teacher Researcher*. Upper Saddle River, NJ: Pearson Education.

Moreno, J. L. 1953. *Who Shall Survive?* New York: Beacon House.

O'Neill, M. S. 2004. *The Effectiveness of Spalding Instruction for Spelling Performance*. Phoenix, AZ: ASU-West, LEE Program in College of Education.

Osgood, C., G. Suci, and P. Tannenbaum. 1957. *The Measurement of Meaning*. Urbana, IL: University of Illinois Press.

Revans, R. W. 1982. *The Origins and Growth of Action Learning*. Lund, Sweden: Studentlitteratur.

Reyes, M. 2004. *The Second Decade: Action Research to Reinvent the California Network of Educational Charters*. Phoenix, AZ: ASU-West, LEE Program of College of Education.

Robertson, E. 1992. "Is Dewey's Educational Vision Still Viable?" In *Review of Research in Education*, edited by G. Grant. Washington, DC: American Educational Research Association.

Sagor, R. 1992. *How to Conduct Collaborative Action Research*. Alexandria, VA: Association for Supervision and Curriculum Development.

———. 2005. *The Action Research Guidebook: A Four-Step Process for Educators and School Teams*. Thousand Oaks, CA: Corwin Press.

Sarason, S. 1990. *The Predictable Failure of Educational Reform*. San Francisco, CA: Jossey-Bass.

Schmuck, R. A. 1968. "Helping Teachers Improve Classroom Group Processes." *Journal of Applied Behavioral Science* 4:401–35.

———, ed. 2000. *Practical Action Research: A Collection of Articles*. Thousand Oaks, CA: Corwin Press.

Schmuck, R. A., M. Chesler, and R. Lippitt. 1966. *Problem Solving to Improve Classroom Learning*. Chicago, IL: Science Research.

Schmuck, R. A. and P. Runkel. 1994. *The Handbook of Organization Development in Schools and Colleges*. 4th ed. Long Grove, IL: Waveland.

Schmuck, R. A. and P. Schmuck. 2001. *Group Processes in the Classroom*. 8th ed. New York: McGraw-Hill.

Schön, D. 1983. *The Reflective Practitioner*. New York: Basic Books.

———. 1987. *Educating the Reflective Practitioner: Toward a New Design for Teaching and Learning in the Professions*. San Francisco, CA: Jossey-Bass.

Scriven, M. 1980. *The Logic of Evaluation*. Inverness, CA: Edge Press.

Sharan, Y. and S. Sharan. 1992. *Expanding Cooperative Learning Through Group Investigation*. New York: Teachers College Press.

Sherman, L., R. A. Schmuck, and P. Schmuck. 2005. *Kurt Lewin's Contribution to the Theory and Practice of Education in the U.S.A.* Bydgoszcz, Poland: Kurt Lewin Center.

Sizer, T. R. 1984. *Horace's Compromise: The Dilemma of the American High School*. Boston, MA: Houghton Mifflin.

———. 1992. *Horace's Compromise: Redesigning the American High School*. Boston, MA: Houghton Mifflin.

Slagle, D. K. 2004. *Action Research to Improve Student Academic Achievement at Westwind Preparatory Academy*. Phoenix, AZ: ASU-West, LEE Program in College of Education.

Spalding, R. B. 2003. *The Writing Road to Reading*. 5th ed. New York: HarperCollins.

Spies, R. A. and B. S. Plake, eds. 2005. *The Sixteenth Mental Measurements Yearbook*. Lincoln, NE: Buros Institute of Mental Measurement, University of Nebraska-Lincoln.

Stringer, E. T. 1996. *Action Research: A Handbook for Practitioners*. Thousand Oaks, CA: Sage.

Taylor, A. E. 1956. *Socrates: The Man and His Thought*. Garden City, NY: Doubleday Anchor.

Taylor, F. W. 1923. *The Principle of Scientific Management*. New York: Harpers.

Thatcher, J. 2004. *Action Research to Develop Formative Assessment Techniques*. Phoenix, AZ: ASU-West, LEE Program in College of Education.

Thelen, H. 1981. *The Classroom Society*. New York: Harsted Press.

Thomas, R. M. 2003. *Blending Qualitative and Quantitative Research Methods in Theses and Dissertations*. Thousand Oaks, CA: Corwin Press.

Thoreau, Henry David. [1854] 1937. *Walden*. New York: Modern Library.

Tileston, D. W. 2005. *Ten Best Teaching Practices*. 2d ed. Thousand Oaks, CA: Corwin Press.

Walker, R. 1985. *Doing Research: A Handbook for Teachers*. London, England: Methuen.

Whyte, W. F. 1943. *Street Corner Society*. Chicago, IL: University of Chicago Press.

———, ed. 1991. *Participatory Action Research*. Newbury Park, CA: Sage.

Index